DEFAULT !!!

Escaping the Debt Trap
and
Avoiding Bankruptcy

By

Heidi Guedel

DEFAULT !!!

Escaping the Debt Trap

and

Avoiding Bankruptcy

By

Heidi Guedel

Please address inquiries to:

H. G. Garofalo

PO Box 1618

Anthony, FL 32617-1618

ISBN: 978-0-557-06620-9

Printed in The United States of America

TABLE OF CONTENTS

PROLOGUE

This is a fact-based novel.

The opening chapter is my fictionalized rendition of the still controversial jury decision handed down before the Justice of the Peace in a humble Common Law court in Credit River Township, Minnesota.

The Credit River case has been one of the primary underpinnings of a continuing monetary protest... a protest predicated on various sources of information concerning the Federal Reserve banking system. Several such sources will be mentioned throughout this book. They are fundamental to the motivations of both myself and my main characters.

What is "Vapor Money"?

The term "Vapor Money" has been gleaned from a variety of sources. To those who have come to believe that the member banks of the Federal Reserve actually create "money out of thin air", it is an accurate metaphor. But to those who still believe that the Federal Reserve banks legitimately lend real money to their borrowers, the term "vapor money" represents a ludicrous, fallacious and unsupportable theory... a theory which they vociferously deny.

In the course of conducting my own research for this novel I participated in a number of lengthy and extremely heated debates on an Internet forum which touts itself as a website dedicated to exposing income tax and monetary frauds and scams.

Chief among such alleged "scams" is the practice of so-called "Debt Elimination"... often referred to as "DE". And the most well-known "DE" promoter, John Gliha, began his career by avoiding the collection of his own unsecured debts. He published a book about his tactics entitled, *"Winning the Collection Game".*

Gliha has also headed up more than one organization which purported to assist debtors in accomplishing the same end. As such he has become quite a target. Another proponent of fighting debt collection is Richard Cornforth. Both their stories (pro and con) and their materials can be found on the Internet.

The couple upon whom I've based this book developed their own tactics after extensive study. They read economics books by Murray N. Rothbard; listened to lectures by Dr. Edwin Vieira, Jr.; read *The Creature From Jekyl Island*, and perused materials by Gliha, and Cornforth. They also obtained encouragement from suijuris.net – a website dedicated to providing support for people legally representing themselves (Pro Se) in Court.

Finally, they purchased tutorial materials from Jurisdictionary.com, which taught them about the process of a typical lawsuit and explained the use and preparation of Motions, legal pleadings and responses.

Their success in avoiding judgment and collection cannot be attributed to any one particular formula... and their story demonstrates the ever-changing nature of this ongoing battle... a battle which is secretly raging... growing... and has been largely ignored by the mainstream media.

In my humble opinion it is the modern-day Boston Tea Party.

My purpose is to bring this information to the attention of a general public which is buckling under the weight of unsecured debt and disconcerted by a so-called Representative Government which has voted (despite overwhelming public protest in 2008) for a shocking, taxpayer-funded, $850 Billion Dollar plus **Bailout** for Wall Street.

Meanwhile many of us on Main Street are being lured into debt, thrown out of foreclosed homes, and forced into ever more punishing forms of bankruptcy in record numbers.

Meanwhile, we hear about the CEOs of bailed-out corporations enjoying all-expense-paid vacations to luxury Spas and retiring with multi-million dollar "Golden Parachutes".

In the author's opinion, this debt-based, Fractional Reserve Lending economy is a disaster and an unconscionable rip-off. Enough is enough.

Heidi Guedel

CHAPTER ONE

Credit River

Bill Drexler cursed and rubbed his half-frozen hands together. He cranked the starter for the umpteenth time and prayed.

It was December 7th, 1968, and 22 degrees below zero in Credit River Township, Minnesota. But he had to make it to court this morning.

One week earlier, the Chief Justice of the Minnesota Supreme Court had called and asked him to act in the capacity of associate Justice of the Peace for this case. No qualified judge except the neighborhood Justice of the Peace, Martin V. Mahoney, had been willing and able to sit on the bench for it. The first two justices were disqualified by Affidavit of Prejudice - the first by the Defendant, and the second by the Plaintiff. A third refused to handle the case. But Justice Mahoney had never supervised a jury trial before, and the Supreme Court Justice thought he could use some support. The motor finally kicked over, and the newly appointed Associate Justice of the Peace scrunched and slipped his way into town... managing to arrive at the makeshift courtroom unscathed.

He arrived about thirty minutes before the commencement of the trial, and helped to build a fire in the wood stove. This trial was to take place in the unheated storeroom of the neighborhood general store. Like the plot device of a Frank Capra movie, these humble men in their unpretentious surroundings were set to preside at the helm of a jury decision that would threaten to rock the nation's banking system and alter the American citizens' concept of the Federal Reserve.

* * *

Lawrence V. Morgan, President of the First National Bank of Montgomery, sat calmly in the witness box while Jerome Daly cross-examined him. After all, he reasoned, it's the truth... we've done nothing wrong.

"Where did the fourteen thousand *dollars* actually **come** from...", Mr. Daly inquired, "...when you funded the account out of which this mortgage loan was issued?"

"Well.. it came from the account we set up on behalf of the borrower... on *your* behalf, Mr. Daly."

"But how did that fourteen thousand dollars actually *arrive* in that account, Mr. Morgan? Where did it *come* from?"

"Well... it was originated by virtue of a bookkeeping entry."

"Are you telling this court, Mr. Morgan, that fourteen thousand dollars just mysteriously appeared in a new account because of a *book*keeping entry?!"

"Well, no... Mr. Daly... not mysteriously at all..."

"Not mysteriously to *you*, perhaps, Mr. Morgan!" The courtroom rippled with nervous laughter. "How exactly is this magical feat accomplished?"

"Magical feat?"

"Yes, Mr. Morgan. Exactly how does your bank cause fourteen thousand dollars to suddenly appear in a new account, out of nowhere, so that I can borrow it and mortgage my land?"

"You signed a loan agreement with us, Mr. Daly, and you promised to pay all of this money back to our bank, with interest."

"I did that, Mr. Morgan. I did indeed. But how did that fourteen thousand dollars wind up in that account from which you loaned it all to *me*?"

"Your mortgage... your promise to repay us that money... allows us to create the account from which that money is loaned."

"And just how is that, Mr. Morgan?"

"Your mortgage loan agreement and your written promise to repay is now an **asset** on our books, and we balance that with a **liability**, which is the money you have borrowed."

"By liability, what exactly do you mean? How is that fourteen thousand dollars a liability now?"

"It is a liability... just like a checking account is a liability to the bank. It has to be paid out on demand... on behalf of its depositor."

*"What **depositor?**"*

"The borrower... in this case, *you*, Mr. Daly."

"Alright. I signed a mortgage with your bank... for fourteen thousand dollars... to buy this piece of land."

"Apparently so, Mr. Daly." A few chuckles bounced around the courtroom in reflex response.

"Then your bank entered my promise to repay you that fourteen thousand dollars ... it entered that mortgage note ... onto the bank's books as an *asset*?"

"That is correct."

"OK. I think we're with you so far. Now your bank needed to spend fourteen thousand dollars to actually give me that loan... am I following you?"

"Correct."

"Well then... where did that money *come* from, Mr. Morgan? What account was debited on your bank's books when that check was issued to the people who sold me that piece of property in 1964?"

"It came from the account which was created when your loan was originated."

"Are you referring to the account that you described earlier as a liability on your books?"

"Exactly."

"So let me understand you, Mr. Morgan. My promise to repay you is an asset on your books, and the money I've borrowed is a corresponding liability?"

"That's right."

"But that liability… that fourteen thousand dollars … did not come from any place else… from out of any other account… into that account that you set up as a liability to balance my promise to repay?"

"No it didn't."

"It didn't what?"

"*What?*"

"It didn't come from out of any *other* bank account into that account you called 'the liability'?"

"That's correct."

"Well just exactly *where* did that money come from then?"

"It was a bookkeeping entry."

"A *bookkeeping* entry???"

"Yes."

"Are you telling this court that in order to loan me fourteen thousand dollars **all** your bank had to do was make a *bookkeeping* entry?"

"Well… it's not quite that simple, Mr. Daly."

"I'm sure it isn't, Mr. Morgan. I'm sure it isn't. If it *were that simple,* we might be tempted to call it **counterfeiting, now wouldn't we!**"

Gasps and nervous laughter… spectators leaned forward in their seats. The jury of twelve squirmed and glanced quickly at each other, then locked their sights back onto the witness. Some were furiously taking notes. The witness crossed and then uncrossed his arms… then wiped both palms off along the tops of his thighs.

"Objection! Immaterial, your Honor! Calls for a conclusion on the part of the witness!" Piped the bank's counsel, Mr. Mellby.

"Please rephrase your question, Mr. Daly." instructed Justice Mahoney.

"Ok... Mr. Morgan... OK. Let me rephrase that. Are you telling this court that the fourteen thousand dollars... this fourteen thousand dollars that you supposedly lent me ... never existed prior to your establishing a liability on your books by virtue of a *bookkeeping* entry?"

"Well, yes, I am. This is standard practice among banks."

"Please clarify for this court what you mean by 'standard practice'."

"I mean that this procedure is standard practice among banks... that we do this in the normal course of our business. We originate funds to lend out in combination with the Federal Reserve Bank of Minneapolis."

"Originate? **Originate?!** Where **was** this money before it was credited to the account that was debited in order to pay the people who sold me that property?

"It did not actually exist prior to your establishing your mortgage with us, Mr. Daly. It came into being as a result of your promissory note – your promise to repay it back to us. The money in the account we set up is actually the money you have promised to repay. We spent it when we paid in advance for your property so that you could repay it to us over a period of time, with interest."

"How can that be? How can the money I've been using to pay you back be in two places at the same time?"

"It can't. It isn't!"

"Wasn't fourteen thousand dollars spent on the purchase of my property in 1964?"

"Yes, it was."

"And haven't I been paying installment payments back to you for four years?"

"Yes, you have, until a few months ago, when you defaulted on that loan and we were forced to foreclose on your property."

"Yes, that's true. But now, are you telling this court that the dollars I've used when I made my monthly payments are the equivalent of the dollars that you paid out to the sellers of my property four years ago?"

"Exactly, Mr. Daly... *exactly!*"

"But didn't that newly originated fourteen thousand dollars go directly to those sellers of that property in the form of a cashier's check drawn on that very account that you set up for this purpose?"

"Yes, it did."

"And what do you suppose those sellers did with their fourteen thousand dollars?"

"I have no idea, Mr. Daly."

"Neither do I. Do you think perhaps they spent that money, Mr. Morgan?"

"I have no idea."

"Do you think they may have put it into their savings account?"

"Perhaps, but I really have no idea."

"But you *do* have some idea that they were able to do with that fourteen thousand dollars as they saw **fit**... right, Mr. Morgan."

"Of course, Mr. Daly."

"Well I **guarantee** that they did **not** see fit to hand it all right back to me so that I could repay it all **right back to you**, Mr. Morgan!" The room erupted in boisterous laughter, and then gradually lapsed into an electrified silence. Mr. Daly circled around his intended prey. Had Jerome Daly been a house cat, the tip of his tail would have twitched and his haunches would have wriggled.

"Now where do you suppose I **did** get the money that I was using to make monthly payments of principal and interest on that so called 'loan' to you, Mr. Morgan?"

"I have no idea."

"We do agree that I did **not** get the money back from the sellers of that property, right, Mr. Morgan."

"Well of course not."

"And we do agree that the money that you... um... *originated* was paid out to the sellers of that property that I bought?"

"Of *course* it was."

"And we must also know that whatever funds that I used in order to make whatever payments that I did make over the last four years came from me... from my savings, from my earnings, or from underneath my mattress... or from wherever... but that money **did** come from me."

"I presume so."

"In any event, it was **not** the very same money that your bank paid out to the sellers of that property."

"Not in the **literal** sense, no... it wasn't the very same dollar bills... of *course* not! How **ridiculous!**" A giggle or two percolated around the room.

"The sellers of that property either still have that money in savings, or under *their* mattress, or they spent it... whatever... but that fourteen thousand dollars is now in circulation. It added to the nation's money supply when you paid it out to those people on my behalf, didn't it?"

"Yes, it did. But it was the same sum, and as the balance of your loan was reduced, the amount owed on that account was reduced accordingly."

"Right, I understand. Your books remained in balance because you reduced the amount I owed you according to the amount of the payments I had made."

"Correct."

"But you originated the sum of fourteen thousand dollars out of thin air, by virtue of a bookkeeping entry, and then spent it by paying it out to the sellers of my property."

"Technically, yes."

"And over the last four years I've made payments to you from funds that I've earned or pulled out of savings… but in any case, it was money that was *already* **in circulation** at the time you originated that fourteen thousand dollars and paid for my property, was it not?"

"I presume so."

"If it wasn't already in circulation, where must it have come from then? I cannot create money for **my**self and use it to pay **my** debts!"

"It was already in circulation."

"Thank you. So the fourteen thousand dollars that you supposedly lent to me was created anew, out of thin air, by a bookkeeping entry, and added to the total overall money supply of the United States of America when it was received by the sellers of my property."

"It was."

"So how can you tell this court, Mr. Morgan, that had I repaid my entire so-called loan to your bank … that the money which you originated would somehow have been eliminated from circulation? Would an army of little gnomes with hats on their heads that read "Bank Loan Funds Recapturing Committee" have run madly around the nation gathering up all fourteen thousand of those dollars from every place where they had been spent or saved up during the last several years… and then returned them to your coffers so that there would be no lasting inflation of the overall money supply, Mr. Morgan?"

"Oh! Don't be *ridiculous!*"

"I agree. Let us **not** be ridiculous. Let us agree for the record that the fourteen thousand dollars that your bank originated by a bookkeeping entry when you funded my so-called 'loan', and then paid out to those people who sold my property to me, is still in circulation."

"I agree."

"And that whatever the sum of money is that I have already managed to remunerate to you over the last four years did not recapture any portion of that original fourteen thousand dollars *back* from circulation... it merely reduced the amount of the debt you say I owe to you... on your books."

"Yes, it has reduced the amount of your outstanding debt on our books... that is what I meant."

"But that entire fourteen thousand dollars that your bank first created with its clever little bookkeeping entry is still out there in circulation, isn't it?"

"Yes it is."

"Thank you. Now...if you were just opening up your bank and no one had yet made a deposit, and I came into your bank, and wanted to take out a loan of $18,000.00, could you loan me that money?"

The Bank President replied, "Yes.", and the jury appeared stunned.

"Does this mean that you can create money out of **thin air?**"

The Bank President said, "Yes. We can create money out of thin air."

"IT SOUNDS LIKE FRAUD TO ME!!!", exclaimed Justice Mahoney, and everyone in that court room nodded their heads in spontaneous agreement.

"So back to my little fourteen thousand dollar mortgage. In what way has your bank risked any of its own money by loaning me this newly created fourteen thousand dollars Mr. Morgan?"

"We have undertaken the business risk of loaning you that money, Mr. Daly."

"Ahhhh. That was quite a serious risk, too, wasn't it? The risk of losing money that you didn't have beforehand anyway... *right* Mr. Morgan? Just exactly what sort of risk is *that?*"

"It is a calculated business risk, as I've said!"

"But what exactly did you have to *lose?*"

"We stood to lose fourteen thousand dollars!"

"Fourteen thousand dollars that you created by virtue of a bookkeeping entry! Fourteen thousand dollars that never existed prior to that bookkeeping entry! Fourteen thousand dollars that you have created out of thin air!"

The courtroom fell silent. People attempted to gather their thoughts. Justice Mahoney felt as if he had followed a white rabbit down a labyrinth and into the bizarre imaginings of Lewis Carroll.

"By what *conceivable* authority do you create money *out of thin air*, Mr. Morgan?!"

"By virtue of the Federal Reserve Act – it's commonly known as 'fractional reserve banking'."

"Thank you, Mr. Morgan… you may step down." Obviously annoyed and somewhat shaken, the President of the First National Bank of Montgomery removed himself from the makeshift witness stand.

By 12:15 PM that same day, a jury of 12 had returned their verdict. Justice Martin V. Mahoney announced it to the awaiting courtroom:

"Now therefore, by virtue of the authority vested in me pursuant to the Declaration of Independence, the Northwest Ordinance of 1787, the Constitution of the United States and the Constitution and the laws of the State of Minnesota not inconsistent therewith, it is hereby ordered, adjudged and decreed:

One - that the Plaintiff is not entitled to recover the possession of Lot 19, Fairview Beach, Scott County, Minnesota according to the Plat thereof on file in the Register of Deeds office.

Two - that because of failure of a lawful consideration the Note and Mortgage dated May 8, 1964 are null and void.

Three - that the Sheriff's sale of the above described premises held on June 26, 1967 is null and void, of no effect.

Four - that the Plaintiff has no right title or interest in said premises or lien thereon as is above described.

Five - that any provision in the Minnesota Constitution and any Minnesota Statute binding the jurisdiction of this Court is repugnant to the Constitution of the United States and to the Bill of Rights of the Minnesota Constitution and is null and void and that this Court has jurisdiction to render complete Justice in this Cause."

Justice Mahoney wrote the following memorandum dated December 9th, 1968:

"The issues in this case were simple. There was no material dispute of the facts for the Jury to resolve.

Plaintiff admitted that it, in combination with the federal Reserve Bank of Minneapolis, which are for all practical purposes, because of their interlocking activity and practices, and both being Banking Institutions Incorporated under the Laws of the United States, are in the Law to be treated as one and the same Bank, did create the entire $14,000.00 in money or credit upon its own books by bookkeeping entry. That this was the Consideration used to support the Note dated May 8, 1964 and the Mortgage of the same date. The money and credit first came into existence when they created it. Mr. Morgan admitted that no United States Law Statute existed which gave him the right to do this. A lawful consideration must exist and be tendered to support the Note. See Ansheuser-Busch Brewing Company v. Emma Mason, 44 Minn. 318, 46 N.W. 558. The Jury found that there was no consideration and I agree. Only God can create something of value out of nothing.

Even if Defendant could be charged with waiver or estoppel as a matter of Law this is no defense to the Plaintiff. The Law leaves wrongdoers where it finds them. See sections 50, 51 and 52 of Am Jur 2nd "Actions" on page 584 – "no action will lie to recover on a claim based upon, or in any manner depending upon, a fraudulent, illegal, or immoral transaction or contract to which Plaintiff was a party."

Plaintiff's act of creating credit is not authorized by the Constitution and Laws of the United States, is unconstitutional and void, and is not a lawful consideration in the eyes of the Law to support any thing or upon which any lawful right can be built.

Nothing in the Constitution of the United States limits the jurisdiction of this Court, which is one of original Jurisdiction with right of trial by Jury guaranteed. This is a Common Law action. Minnesota cannot limit or impair the power of this Court to render Complete Justice between the parties. Any provisions in the Constitution and laws of Minnesota which attempt to do so is repugnant to the Constitution of the United States and void. No question as to the Jurisdiction of this Court was raised by either party at the trial. Both parties were given complete liberty to submit any and all facts to the Jury, at least in so far as they saw fit.

No complaint was made by Plaintiff that Plaintiff did not receive a fair trial. From the admissions made by Mr. Morgan the path of duty was direct and clear for the Jury. Their Verdict could not reasonably have been otherwise. Justice was rendered completely and without denial, promptly and without delay, freely and without   purchase, conformable to the laws in this Court of December 7, 1968.

BY THE COURT
December 9, 1968
Justice Martin V. Mahoney
Credit River Township

Note: It has never been doubted that a Note given on a Consideration which is prohibited by law is void. It has been determined, independent of Acts of Congress, that sailing under the license of an enemy is illegal. The emission of Bills of Credit upon the books of these private Corporations for the purpose of private gain is not warranted by the Constitution of the United States and is unlawful. See Craig v. Mo. 4 Peters Reports

912.   This Court can tread only that path which is marked out by duty.   M.V.M."

* * *

Jerome Daly left the improvised courtroom in apparent triumph. The members of that jury felt as if they had made history. Justice Mahoney was determined to take this decision and predicate other decisions upon it, in the interests of truth and justice.

He believed that the Federal Reserve was crooked, and that America's paper Federal Reserve notes were worthless.

When the bank attempted to appeal this decision, they tendered the two-dollar fee in Federal Reserve notes, and Justice Mahoney refused to accept them as lawful payment for their appeal. They could have tendered two silver dollars and Justice Mahoney would have accepted those as lawful payment. They could have tendered four silver half-dollars, or eight silver quarters, or twenty silver dimes, or any combination thereof that totaled two dollars in United States coinage... but they refused.

Rather than honor the Justice of the Peace's opinion that Federal Reserve notes were worthless, and pay for their appeal in hard money, the bank's representatives failed to pay within the statutory time allotted, and the case was never overturned or upheld by a higher court.

Enlivened by this apparent precedent, attorney Jerome Daly - the former debtor-turned-victor - proceeded to round up clients who also wanted to absolve themselves of their mortgage debt using the same argument. Justice of the Peace Mahoney was ready and willing to sit on those cases, too. Both men felt empowered to expose this apparent banking and lending fraud before the American people and the world.

Bill Drexler wrote, in part:

> *"The Credit River Decision, handed down by a jury of 12 on a cold day in December, in the Credit River Township, was an experience that I'll never forget.*
>
> *I must admit that up until that point, I really didn't believe Jerome's theory. And thought he was making this up. After I heard the testimony of the banker, my mouth had*

dropped open in shock, and I was in complete disbelief. There was no doubt in my mind that the jury would find for Daly.

Jerome Daly had taken on the banks, the Federal Reserve Banking System, and the money lenders, and had won.

Both Jerome Daly and Martin V. Mahoney, Justice of the Peace, are truly the "greatest men that I've ever had the pleasure to meet." The Credit River Decision was and still is the most important legal decision ever decided by a jury.

Bill Drexler"

On December 27th, 1968, Jerome Daly wrote a letter to Mr. Patrick Foley, United States Attorney for Minnesota, which said, in part:

"If any Appellate Court, including the Supreme Court of the United States, in review of this Judgment, perpetrates a fraud upon the People by defying the Constitutional Law of the United States, Mahoney has resolved that he will convene another Jury in Credit River Township to try the issue of the fraud on the part of any State or Federal Judge. And in an action on my part to recover the possession, if the Jury decides in my favor, the Constable and the Citizens Militia of Credit River Township will, pursuant to the Law, deliver me back into possession. So you see, this Justice of the Peace can keep the peace in Scott County, Minnesota, not with the help of these State and Federal Judges who have fled reality, but in spite of them. This Thomas Jefferson's Prophesy with reference to Chattel Slavery once again rings true: "God's Justice will not sleep forever."

Shortly thereafter, Jerome Daly took it upon himself to defend a group of three men accused of counterfeiting Federal Reserve notes. They were acquitted, based upon Mr. Daly's defense arguments alleging that the Federal Reserve notes had no more intrinsic value than the counterfeit notes. The jury apparently agreed.

His next move was to represent another debtor, Leo Zurn, against one Roger D. Derrick and the Northwestern National Bank of Minneapolis. But before Daly could sink another ball in the side pocket with Justice Martin V. Mahoney presiding, the Supreme Court of Minnesota stepped in.

On July 11th, 1969, Justice C. Donald Peterson, acting for the Minnesota Supreme Court, directed Mr. Daly and Justice Mahoney to Show Cause why they should not be permanently restrained from further proceedings in the Justice Court.

Justice Peterson ordered a stay of all further proceedings before the Justice of the Peace pending final determination of the questions raised by Northwestern National Bank's petition for writ of prohibition. The mere existence of this action by the Supreme Court was intended to halt Daly and Mahoney in their juggernaut against the banks and the monetary system. But they pressed on.

On July 14th. 1969, Justice Mahoney, upon Motion by Mr. Daly, entered findings of fact, conclusions of law, and an order for judgment in favor of Leo Zurn against the Northwestern National Bank of Minneapolis.

On August 21st, 1969, Jerome Daly appeared on behalf of himself and Justice Mahoney, in response to another Order to Show Cause why they should not be held in 'constructive contempt' of the Supreme Court of Minnesota for this conduct. Mr. Daly acknowledged before the Court that both he, and the Justice of the Peace, intentionally violated the order of Justice Peterson... because, in their opinion, neither the Supreme Court of Minnesota nor Justice Peterson had Jurisdiction to issue it.

The very next day, August 22nd, 1969, Justice of the Peace Martin V. Mahoney was dead.

The Eagle, a newspaper in Yakima, Wash., reported in its issue of September 11th, 1969:

"Whether he was given a whiff of prussic acid or handed a fatal cigarette is not known at this time, but the

possibility is certainly more than idle speculation. The international conspiracy, which owns and controls our Federal Reserve System, and which has brought our nation to the brink of the most cataclysmic financial crash in history, is understandably unhappy with the earthy judge whose name is Mahoney. The case and its outcome has sent quivers and spasms up and down the entire trunk lines and tentacles of the conspiracy as literally thousands of people across the nation have challenged the duplicity of the king-makers over the thievery of their hard-earned wealth."

After Justice Mahoney's convenient and timely death, the powers that be continued their pursuit and punishment of Mr. Daly.

On September 5th, 1969, the Supreme Court of Minnesota held Jerome Daly in contempt for advising the late Justice of the Peace to disregard an Order of the Supreme Court. He was suspended from practicing law, pending further proceedings to determine if more severe measures should be taken against him. In that proceeding, the Supreme Court noted, in paragraph [33]:

"(6) … We are satisfied from the record that the Justice of the Peace acted upon the advice and at the instance of attorney Jerome Daly…The fact that such advice is prompted by fanciful notions that Justice of the Peace courts have a constitutional status giving them immunity from the jurisdiction of the supreme court of this state cannot excuse or justify this conduct."

On November 14th, 1969, the Supreme Court of Minnesota disbarred Jerome Daly. He was no longer permitted to practice law. Any proceedings in the Justice Court presided over by Martin V. Mahoney following August 15th, 1969 were declared a "nullity". That encompassed exactly seven days prior to Mahoney's death on August 22nd 1969.

To this day, that first, astounding, and landmark decision at Credit River Township remains a fact as well as a legend. It has not been nullified, but it cannot be cited as authority in subsequent cases because it was never confirmed by a higher State Court of Appeal, either.

And the testimony of Bank President Lawrence V. Morgan cannot be quoted or relied upon as authority in any other case which does not directly involve The First National Bank of Montgomery itself because it would be ruled out as inadmissible hearsay.

So present day legal opinion appears to concur – whether the testimony involved was true or not, this case doesn't seem to matter any more. It has seemingly been buried along with its Justice of the Peace............

CHAPTER TWO
The Lure...

Brooke was a talented woman. She had been a professional artist for over 25 years. But today she was relegated to the task of juggling credit card balances.

Recently, she and her husband, Hawley, had been receiving numerous offers in the mail... 90% of them from the same four credit card companies: FunniBank; Capital One; American Express, and Bank One.

For the last two months three out of four of these companies had included so called "convenience checks" along with their monthly statements. A friendly and upbeat letter was enclosed, informing Brooke and/or her husband that these checks could be utilized for the purpose of transferring higher interest balances over from other credit card companies. After transfer, these balances would then be charged zero interest for a period of six months to one year.

In smaller print, elsewhere among these several pages of tempting information, she found the sentences which informed her that **although** any newly transferred balance would indeed be charged zero interest for the period of time specified in the offer, the *already* existing balance on the account would remain there at its current rate of interest until the recently transferred balance had been paid off **first**.

Suddenly her head began to pound and a knot formed in the muscle tissue adjacent to her left shoulder blade. Taking a deep breath she told herself to calm down and think about this for a minute.

She took all four of the monthly statements out of their envelopes and arranged them in front of herself on the dining room table. On one of these accounts she and her husband had run up over $26,000.00 in debt. On another account, they had run up over $10,000.00. The other two were relatively new, and each had less than $1,000.00 owing.

A strategy began to dawn on her. First, she would transfer the small balances into the accounts which already carried the larger balances. That would leave two of the accounts empty. And since the two accounts with the smaller balances had sent them convenience checks, she would wait to use those convenience checks until each of those two accounts was empty.

Immediately thereafter, she would use their convenience checks to transfer the $26,000.00 balance into one of the newly emptied accounts and the $10,000.00 balance into the other. That way there would be no pre-existing balances in either of those accounts being charged any 15% for at least the next six months.

She also found the little sentence informing her that any new purchases made on these credit cards would be charged the normal rate of interest... but that any monthly payments made from that point on would be credited against the transferred balance(s) first.

"Wait a minute ...", she thought out loud, *"...this means that the zero interest stuff gets paid off first while the higher interest stuff sits there for a much longer time."*

"OK. Clear your head and sort this out."

"You're going to transfer all of the money you owe into two of these four accounts, thereby emptying the other two."

"Then you're going to move all of the money back out of these two and into the two accounts that you've just emptied out. Right! Good!"

"Then if you have to buy anything else, you're going to charge it on one of the two empty accounts."

"Then when you make your monthly payments, you will be paying against any new charges while you are also paying

against the big balances that will now only be charged 0% for the next several months. That should give us enough time to get back on our feet."

Just to make absolutely certain that she didn't confuse herself and forget what she had just managed to figure out, Brooke grabbed a scratch pad and wrote out this plan step by step.

Then she walked over to the roll top desk, pulled out their checkbook and wrote out this month's minimum payment for each of the two accounts containing the largest amount of debt. The two smaller accounts were going to be cleaned out and transferred using the convenience checks offered by the first two banks. She felt a little bit light-headed because this way, a little bit less money was being written out of their checking account this month.

She made doubly certain that she was putting the correct checks in the appropriate envelopes, licked them, closed them, and added the stamps and the nice little return address stickers that she and her husband always received from the Disabled American Veterans association.

Then she slumped back in the dining room chair and stared at the billing statements scattered in front of her. She usually wrote each monthly payment check one at a time, soon after it arrived. This was the first time that she had seen them all at once. *"How in hell did we manage to run up all of this debt?",* she groaned.

* * *

Brooke wasn't used to being a housewife. For 25 years of her adult life she had been a reasonably successful better-than-average professional artist. She honestly conceived of herself as only "better-than-average". After all, once she'd graduated out of her hometown grammar school where she had been recommended into a special extracurricular art class for gifted students, and had later graduated from high school where she'd won Art awards and earned straight A's in each of her yearly art classes... she had moved into a realm of excellence at companies where every artist at the studio was probably the best in their own hometown. These studios were the first real challenge that Brooke had ever felt as an artist... a little fish in some very big ponds.

But now she felt an equally unfamiliar challenge, and much more uncomfortable for her. None of the familiar studios for whom she had worked for several years apiece were interested in employing her. She was a *traditional* artist ... the kind who creates with a paper and pencil. Over 300 of her former colleagues had been laid off in California and a similar number had been drop-kicked from her studio's facilities in Florida.

"No one wants to see traditional art work anymore!", they told her. "Everybody wants to see 3-D imagery... like *Toy Story* and *Shrek!* And besides, you're over 50. We don't want to retrain *you* when dozens of new young 3-D artists are graduating from art schools all over the country. Sorry."

Brooke felt bad enough for herself, but she knew a couple who had *both* worked at one of the studios and neither one of them had a job anymore. They had two children in college. "I wonder how *they're* doing now.", she thought. She had lost touch with most of her colleagues when 'the music stopped' and all of them scrambled for the few remaining chairs at the few remaining desks at the few remaining traditional studio jobs in their dwindling industry. Now she felt so damned alone.

* * *

Her husband was at work earning a modest salary at a very demanding position with the County Department of Children and Families. He had graduated summa cum laude with a master's degree in marriage and family therapy, but he could only find a salaried position doing social work for the county.

They were both disappointed in the current state of their careers... both talented people who were used to achieving... both bearing up under a mutual midlife crisis... and now they had run up all this damned debt.

When Brooke had worked for the studios all those years she and Hawley became used to having plenty of money. They paid all their bills on time. They took pride in refusing to run up the two or three credit cards which they kept for convenience. They didn't like having to carry cash, and personally, Brooke always enjoyed the oh-so-friendly letters of temptation from all of those credit card companies vying for their business.

She loved it whenever there was an occasion to check their credit rating. She knew it was excellent. It felt like a form of personal validation. And their credit score was still exceptional. They had never missed a payment. No payment had ever been late.

But now the payments were exceeding her husband's take-home pay, and for the first time in her adult life, Brooke was bringing home nothing. She was watching their savings slowly dissipate with every round of monthly minimum payments to those four credit card accounts. Hence, this desperate little juggling act with those "convenience checks".

Now she saw the wolves on the doorstep. She kept envisioning various scenarios.

After their savings had dwindled away and her husband's income could no longer support both their ordinary monthly living expenses and these minimum monthly credit card payments, what would happen next? They would have to stop making the credit card payments.

And what about the car payments? One of their cars was leased. It was a mini-van that Hawley drove to work every day. He had to drive all over the county visiting Foster families and checking up on the welfare of the children in each of those homes. It already had over 90,000 miles on it.

Brooke was earning her real estate broker's license in an attempt to become a financially productive member of their marital partnership once again. She had held onto a small motor home that Hawley's parents had helped them to purchase. It was intended to be her mobile real estate office. Not officially of course … state law prohibited any real estate office except one that was located at a permanent address… but it would function as a wonderful little rolling office just the same.

How could they pull themselves back up by the bootstraps and meet their financial obligations if they lost their vehicles to the creditors?

Brooke conceived of another desperate plan. The next time they received any of those zero interest balance transfer offers from any of those credit card companies she would transfer everything they owed against both of those vehicles onto the credit card accounts.

She knew what she was doing. She knew that one day soon she and her husband might no longer be able to feed themselves, maintain their home, and make those minimum monthly credit card payments. She knew that Florida was a 100% homestead protection state. She also knew that only Texas and Florida protected their citizens 100% from the seizure of their principal residence for payment of debt. She knew that the only debts which could be leaned against their homesteaded residence were taxes.

No matter what, she and Hawley had to have enough money on hand to pay their income taxes and their property taxes or else they could lose their home. If she waited any longer to take these steps the little savings they still retained would be eaten up in credit card payments, and they would still go bankrupt.

A couple of months later, some more tempting letters from credit card companies with more zero interest balance transfer convenience checks arrived in the mail. Brooke took a deep breath, pulled out the paperwork for both of their automobile loans and spread it all out on the table.

Because of their excellent payment history she and her husband had been offered higher and higher credit limits. Each of these four credit card companies had upped their credit card spending limit to between $25,000 and $30,000. Brooke felt like a pathetic, miserable thief... but she still wrote out one of those convenience checks for enough money to pay off the van, and the other one for enough money to pay off all but the last few thousand dollars that they owed on the little motor home.

The balance transfers left in the United States mail the next morning. By the end of the month they owned the pink slip on the van, and would not have to make another payment on the motor home for three more years.

Brooke lapsed slowly into a persistent depression. Although she was making excellent grades in her real estate broker's class she still felt like a loser. Hawley was such a good soldier and such a responsible husband. Dutifully he went off to work every day and his paychecks were automatically deposited in their joint checking account.

And what was Brooke doing? Desperately shuffling money around from credit card to credit card like a carnival performer pulling the 'find the little green pea under the walnut shells' act. She felt like a useless piece of crap.

She used to earn $100,000.00 a year. They used to keep all of their credit cards paid off every single month. They took pride in it...but not anymore.

Every now and then Hawley would pace around the living room in a state of agitation, complaining about the fact that they had run up all of those credit cards, and how this was so against his personal ethics.

Meanwhile those tempting little balance transfer letters just kept filling up the mailbox day after day after day. Only now they were sometimes accompanied by other letters inquiring as to whether or not Brooke and Hawley would like to apply for a home equity line of credit in order to pay off all of this annoying credit card debt.

But Brooke knew better than to mortgage their homestead in order to pay off unsecured credit card debt.

She had managed to purchase her first home when she was working at her first studio job 30 years ago. She lived there for a few years, made her mortgage payments, survived the collapse of her first marriage and subsequent divorce, profited from an appreciation in value on that first little house, and paid cash for the next one.

She had religiously avoided mortgaging her principle residence ever since. She owned her own home outright when she met her husband, Hawley.

When the 2-D art business dropped the floor out from under her, the two of them decided that they could no longer afford to live in California. They relocated to Florida. Now they lived in a 100% homestead protection state. There was no way they were ever going to willingly mortgage their home.

Every now and then Brooke would catch one of those Internet loan companies' television advertisements. One of them depicted a seemingly euphoric loan customer throwing a slew of credit cards into his back yard wood chipper and exclaiming with great delight what a relief it was to have mortgaged his house in order to pay off those credit cards. Brooke never failed to make a wry remark about how foolish that guy in the commercial was. She believed that with all her heart.

Now... clearly seeing the wolves on the doorstep... she sat down at their computer, logged onto the Internet and began to research the topic of bankruptcy.

That desperate but seemingly innocuous move would set in motion a series of events to forever change both their lives.

CHAPTER THREE
Into the Net

It was 2:00 in the morning and Brooke's eyelids felt like sandpaper when she blinked. She'd been having trouble sleeping anyway... she might as well make good use of the time she used to spend squirming impatiently in bed and trying not to awaken Hawley, who had to get his sleep on a work night.

So she sat in front of their computer, further researching the astounding topic of "debt elimination". That's right – **elimination**. Unbelievable. How could anyone just make their debts "go away" with impunity? This had to be 'too good to be true'. But she kept right on reading.

She had intended to do research on bankruptcy, but along with the assortment of reference materials pertaining to bankruptcy, these two websites touting debt elimination turned up.

Apparently the key word "bankruptcy" was linked to the debt elimination web sites as well. No wonder... both of the elimination sites elaborated at great length about what a poor choice bankruptcy was. One of the debt elimination sites displayed the Better Business Bureau logo.

"Well..." thought Brooke, "...THAT certainly lends an air of legitimacy to the whole thing!"

Just to make absolutely sure she wasn't falling for some Internet scam, she clicked on the "BBB" logo and checked up on the debt elimination company. The BBB reported that <u>Alternative Debt Services</u> had been in business for almost five years. Under the heading "Nature of Business" appeared: "This is an alternative to bankruptcy. This is a specialty company that offers assistance in eliminating debt." It had a clean record… so back to the <u>Alternative Debt Services</u> site she went.

Back at the ADS website, Brooke read through the Frequently Asked Questions:

"Q. What is your guarantee?

1. The member must follow the strategies of The Debt Termination Program. The joint accounts of married couples are guaranteed the same as for individuals.

2. The resolution of the disputed account must be in any state of the United States of America.

3. The member must cooperate with our customer service and follow our program guidelines exactly. Each member agrees to allow us, and our affiliates to publish the results of each collection within the limits of any settlement agreements.

4. As long as client's debt qualifies, (major credit card, Visa, Mastercard, unsecured loan, or any other debt with approval from ADS), and client follows the program exactly as laid out in the Debt Termination Program, with or without support, as well as completes the program from start to finish, if the program does not work, ADS will provide client with a 100% money back guarantee. If any client does not follow the above criteria or does not put forth the effort to complete the program and provide the necessary assistance to the "Workgroup", if applicable, client will not qualify to receive the satisfaction guarantee."

"Q. How does your debt termination program work?

A. It is a 100% legal, proprietary process designed to close your credit card accounts and cancel your unsecured debts without you having to pay the balances."

"Q. Have you had a lot of success with it?

A. Yes. We have applied the program to literally thousands of collection cases   since 1994 and have stopped hundreds of millions of dollars from being collected. We're the only company in the industry with the success and true (case work) experience."

"Q. Can you help me if I already have a judgment and/or a garnishment because of the judgment?

A. Yes, so far our program has been able to reverse these types of judgments and recover all of the money garnished and clear the credit history as part of the process."

"Q. What other benefits does your program offer?

A. No other organization has this program, or anything like it. No other organization has the professional support to handle the case work and negotiating through paralegals, certified public accountants and attorneys. No other organization guarantees that if the program does not work, they will refund your money. You can avoid the invasive nature of bankruptcy and be selective over which accounts you want to terminate. Our strategies allow you to keep some of your credit accounts while terminating others."

Brooke was now 99% convinced. She ignored that persistent little 1% that kept hopping up and down in her mind waving its bright red flag.

She filled out the contact form on the web site and left their home telephone number and e-mail address. Within 24 hours a representative of ADS called her. As always, she screened the incoming call.

"Hello, this message is for Brooke Martin. My name is Albert Gonzalez and I am calling in response to the contact form you filled out on our debt elimination website…" She grabbed it before he could hang up. *"Might as well grab it on his dime…"* she thought. No more concept of having plenty of money to live on. Every penny counted now.

"Yes! This is Brooke Martin. Thank you for calling back so quickly!" her apparent eagerness was no surprise to Albert. *"All of these debtors are desperate…"* he reflected, silently. "…this should be another easy mark."

"You can take a deep breath and start to relax now, my dear. You have made your last credit card payment." There was a pause while Brooke gathered her thoughts. "Are you still there?" queried Albert.

"Yes… yes… I'm still here. I just don't see how it could possibly be quite that easy." she replied in that strange little froggy voice which always seemed to take over when she became at all unsure of herself. She hated it, but there was really nothing she could do about it… never had been.

"Well it is an involved process… I won't kid you about it.", he continued. His voice seemed warm… almost fatherly. "There is a detailed, step-by-step process that you have to follow exactly the way we tell you. If you do that, you have our money back guarantee."

"Is it legal?"

"Oh yes! Absolutely!"

"OK…oh…oh……ok…" she stammered. "Please go over it with me."

"Alright. What you will be doing… with our help, and with our materials that we will provide to you… is that you will be initiating a bona fide dispute with all of your credit card companies."

"What grounds do we have to dispute anything?"

"The fact that none of these credit card companies ever really lent you any money!"

"You're KIDDING!!!"

"Nope. It's the God's honest truth!"

"Well, then, who paid for all the stuff we bought with all those credit cards?"

"YOU did!"

"What?!"

"Yep… when you promised to pay back the purchase price with interest."

"But didn't the bank pay for it all, and now we're supposed to reimburse them?"

"That's what you've always thought isn't it?"

"Well… *sure* it is!"

"Well, it's **not** the truth!"

"How do you **know** that?"

"Because the bankers admit it themselves, if you know where to look." Brooke listened in stunned silence as Albert continued his explanation.

"Right there on the Federal Reserve websites are several different articles describing the way that the banks create money out of thin air when they lend credit. First, they take your written agreement… your promise to pay them the money back… and they enter that on their books as an asset."

"Why is that an asset?"

"Because it amounts to money that they expect to **receive**… even if it is over a period of time. So it's an asset. Then, to make sure that their books balance they create a liability."

"What do you mean?"

"It's a liability for the same reason that a customer's checking account is a liability. It is money that the bank is obligated to pay **out**.

Your promise to pay the money back is an **asset** because it is money that the bank expects to be paid **in**. But the liability is a balance on deposit from which the customer can take money **out** upon demand.

Whenever you charge something on your credit card, that money is debited out of that liability account and credited to the merchants that you bought stuff from.

The thing is that the bank never actually put any money into that liability account. The bank just set it up according to the credit spending limit they decided to give you… made a bookkeeping entry to indicate that there was that much money in the account and then debited that account whenever they paid a merchant on your behalf.

They created money out of thin air by making a bookkeeping entry to counterbalance the asset that they claimed when you signed a paper promising that you would pay the money back."

"But if I promised to pay it back, how can I get out of that promise?"

"Didn't you promise to pay back money that they lent you?"

"Yes..."

"Well they didn't really lend you **anything.** They didn't put any of **their** money into that liability account. They used your promise to pay the money back as an asset on their books to counterbalance the money that they created out of thin air when they set up your credit card account. They deposited your promise to pay the same way a person would deposit a check. You know a check is just a promise to pay money out of someone's account right?"

"Right..."

"And when you deposit a check from someone else into your checking account, your account is credited for the same amount that the check-writer's account is debited, right?"

"Right..."

"Well, when your promise to repay is deposited by the bank, and that liability account is created, no other account is debited. That money came out of nowhere. The bank did not use its own pre-existing funds to put that money into that account from out of any other account... so they did not advance you any of their own money to pay for anything you bought with your credit card.

They just used your promise to pay like a check, and they deposited it without ever having to spend anything of their own to pay the merchants you bought stuff from. So why should you repay them anything? They didn't **spend** anything?"

"They spent the money that I promised to pay back to them."

"Yes they did. But normally, when someone lends money to you, they have to pull it out of their own pocket, or out of their own bank account, or they have to sell something they own in order to get it… but they take money of their own and lend it to you to spend. Then you pay it back to them with interest, so they can make some extra money **for taking the risk of lending you their money** in the first place.

But the way the banks did these credit card accounts, they never had to spend any of their own money, so what kind of **risk** did they take? **None!**"

"So the merchants got paid with money that never existed before? Money I agreed to pay back, without the bank ever having to pay it out first?"

"Yep."

Brooke took a deep breath and tried to digest what she had just heard. Again, she thought of a carnival barker switching around those three little half walnut shells while she tried unsuccessfully to keep her eye on the one with a green pea underneath.

Albert broke into her mental imagery after a moment or two. "I'm going to suggest a book for you to read. "*The Creature From Jekyll Island*", by Griffin. I think it will help you to understand."

"OK… great… thanks..." Brooke felt dumbfounded.

"You get yourself a copy and read it and then call me back if you have any further questions."

"OK… I will… thanks again Albert. Bye for now."

She hung up the telephone, went right over to her computer and ordered the book through Amazon.com. It arrived within two weeks. It took her another week to read it… but she would never see the world of international banking, or money lending the same way again.

In fact she had never really thought much about banking and/or banking procedures before. She was an artist… not an accountant.

Just to be certain that she really understood what she had been reading, she searched the net for other authorities on banking. She found an author by the name of Murray N. Rothbard, now deceased, who had written 26 books on the

Federal Reserve banking system and economics... including two which really seemed to intrigue her: "*The Case Against the Fed*", and "*What Has Government Done to Our Money*?"

After she had read all three of these books, Brooke felt entitled to pursue the debt elimination process.

Each of these sources described the very same process of creating money out of thin air, and devaluing the purchase power of the dollar by causing rampant inflation. It certainly seemed like fraud to *her!*

Outraged, she called up Alternative Debt Services and spoke to Albert again. It cost her and Hawley $2,500.00 to purchase the debt elimination program... and they had just enough room to charge this amount on one of their remaining credit cards.

* * *

Within a couple of days Brooke received an e-mail from the "Workgroup" at ADS. It contained a whole series of dispute letters which were to be dispatched to each of the credit card companies.

The first letter was to include a $20.00 check made out to the bank and identified within the accompanying letter as both a final payment on that credit card account and consideration for an agreement to arbitrate. The letter said very clearly that cashing the $20.00 check would represent their acceptance of consideration in connection with the agreement to arbitrate. And the agreement was to submit the bank to binding arbitration in a forum to be chosen by the *customers* ... not the "pet" arbitration companies that were always specified by the banks.

Brooke pulled out all of the paperwork and observed that each of these credit card issuing banks had included an arbitration clause in their cardholder agreements. The cardholder agreements all stated that if the customer used the credit card, the customer had thereby agreed to all of the conditions and stipulations of the cardholder agreement.

So how could Brooke and Hawley avoid being forced into arbitration with one of the two companies that these credit card holder agreements had specified? Suddenly she felt a wave of heat rise through her body and nervous perspiration appeared on her forehead. Her heart pounded. She rifled through the ADS paperwork, found their telephone number, and called Albert again.

"How does this letter and this $20.00 check make the bank accept a different arbitration company? Our using their credit card is supposed to make us use one of *their* arbitration companies?"

"Because… if they cash your $20.00 check they have accepted the consideration that you provided for a **new** agreement. The new agreement supersedes the old agreement … **as long as you never again use that credit card**."

Within minutes she felt completely reassured. She thanked Albert very warmly and returned to the task of customizing and preparing all of those dispute letters for mailing.

This series of letters, in and of itself, provided quite an education for Brooke. The letters incorporated numerous reference materials pertaining to Federal Reserve banking, including several written reports which had actually been authored by employees of the Federal Reserve… both past and present.

In each case these reference materials contained a description of this so-called process of money creation "out of thin air".

"My GOD! Why have they been allowed to do this for so long?" she exclaimed aloud… although no one was present to hear her. *"What have I stumbled **into?**"* She took off her glasses and ran her left hand through her short dark hair.

Then she got up and went into the kitchen. There were two large chocolate bars stashed in the pantry. She ate one of them.

* * *

When Hawley got home from work she tried to catch him up on all of this detailed information. But after a certain point he just shook his head and waved his hands back and forth as if he was driving away a cloud of gnats.

"I'm sorry sweetheart. I've just got so much on my mind pertaining to my work with children and foster families... I... I just cannot digest this right now." He appeared distressed and overwhelmed.

She remembered all of those times that he had paced back and forth complaining about the amount of debt they had racked up, and the size of the monthly payments they were making.

It's not that he blamed *her*. Each of them realized that they had participated in this fiasco together, believing that their dual career household afforded them the security to purchase things on credit. They often laughed about the acronym that was applied to their kind of marriage: DINKs, they were called: Dual Income, No Kids. Neither of them had ever expected Brooke's lucrative career to collapse out from under her. What in the hell could they do *now?*

There was a time when neither one of them would ever have **dreamt** of stiffing four credit card companies, let alone one! It was unthinkable!

They'd have talked about selling their house and some of their furniture or one of their cars. They'd have planned to move into a smaller house or to a different state where property would be less expensive.

But not now. Not after reading **"The Creature From Jekyll Island"**, and **"What Has Government Done to Our Money?"** and **"The Case Against the Fed"**.

Now they both believed that the whole country had been duped and ripped off by the Federal Reserve banks and all those wealthy clandestine banking families and their carefully contrived cartel.

How could Congress allow such a thing to happen?

* * *

As the next several weeks passed, a couple of the credit card issuing banks sent letters back to the Martins. None of these letters addressed the actual issues raised in the dispute, but offered a sort of general defense based upon the Martin's use of the credit card:

"Dear Mr. and Mrs. Martin:

Thank you for your correspondence to the executive offices of _____ bank. I have been asked to respond on their behalf and I welcome this opportunity to address your concerns.

Please know that our banking procedures regarding unsecured lines of credit have been designed to accommodate all of our customers as well as, protect the interest of _____ bank. I can assure you that _____ bank complies with all regulatory agencies governing our business.

The Cardmember Agreement clearly states that the acceptance of the Card, which is signified by its presentation and use, is acceptance's of the full terms of the Cardmember Agreement. Therefore, the Basic Cardmember is bound by the Cardmember Agreement, and is contractually liable to make all payments on time. If payments are not made according to the Cardmember Agreement, _____ bank reserves the right to report the account as delinquent to any and all credit reporting agencies. Please be advised, any further correspondence regarding this issue will be filed without response.

In light of the above referenced information a zero balance statement will not be forthcoming, as the balance is valid by usage of the Card. Once the balance is paid to zero, the Basic Cardmember may request a zero balance letter.

Sincerely,

(Stamped, unintelligible Signature)

Executive Assistant

And:

RE: Account No: XXXX XXXX XXXX XXXX

Dear Brooke Martin:

As a national banking institution, we are regulated by – and comply with – all applicable Federal and state laws. When you accepted the credit card account noted above, you made an honorable agreement to accept the terms and conditions in the Cardmember Agreement you received when the account was initially opened and amended, thereafter. This Cardmember Agreement represents a contractual obligation expressly stating that the Cardmember promises to pay for all purchases and cash advances made by the Cardmember or authorized persons.

Please be advised that, in accordance with the terms noted in this agreement, the bank has elected to close your account. As you are aware, your credit card account number, listed above, was opened in ___ of 1998. It currently reflects a balance of $_____. Payments were received until ____, 2004.

Your use of the account signifies your acceptance of the terms and conditions associated with the account. The debt will not be forgiven or intimidated.

Sincerely,

Stamped, unintelligible Signature

Financial Services Advisor

Brooke followed up with each of these banks by sending a letter reiterating the issues brought up in the original letters of dispute:

RE: NOTICE OF DISPUTE;

Account No. XXXX XXXX XXXX XXXX

Greetings:

I have recently made an inquiry with your company concerning the above referenced account. I have become aware that your company used my credit application or note to originate funds which did not exist prior to my application. I am aware that you did not risk or lose any money at any time, yet you were unjustly enriched from fees and interest paid to you by myself and by merchants. I am disputing every charge or debit to this account.

This Notice is made pursuant to 15 USC § 1666(a). 12 CFR 226.13(a), which states that the term "billing error" includes, in part:

"(5) A reflection on a periodic statement of <u>a computational or similar error of an accounting nature that is made by the creditor</u>."

"(6) A reflection on a periodic statement of an extension of credit for which <u>the consumer requests additional clarification, including documentation evidence</u>." (Emphasis added.)

I assert that the true and complete terms were never disclosed to me. However, if you disagree with the assertions herein, you are permitted to do one of the following:

1. Mail or deliver to the consumer an explanation that sets forth the reasons for the creditor's belief that the billing error alleged by the consumer is incorrect in whole or in part;

2. Furnish copies of documentary evidence of the consumer's indebtedness, if the consumer so requests; and

3. If a different billing error occurred, correct the billing error and credit the consumer's account with any disputed amount and related finance or other charges, as applicable.

If you fail, neglect, or refuse to acknowledge this notice within thirty (30) days, or make appropriate corrections or send a written explanation within ninety (90) days, as prescribed by the Fair Credit Billing Act, I may elect to file a complaint with the FTC and the Attorney General in my home state (where you conduct business) and/or seek other legal recourse.

I am requesting:

A) An authenticated front and back copy of the alleged original agreement, in full (full and complete disclosure);

B) An authenticated front and back copy of all documents and records, including but not limited to any and all Promissory Notes, money equivalents or similar instruments, identified as or evidencing assets provided by and/or signed by the consumer;

C) An identification of the source of the funds used to fund the charges, including account name(s), number(s), and amount(s);

D) The name and address of the Custodian(s) of Records of all relevant documents and accounts;

E) A statement of the total amount of all payments made by the consumer.

Sincerely, Brooke Martin"

This communiqué was never acknowledged. Instead, Brooke received the following unsigned response from one of the four banks:

"Dear Cardmember:

Our records indicate that we have previously responded to the concerns expressed in your most recent letter. We also believe that our previous response adequately addressed those concerns. Please be advised that future inquiries, which reflect the same concerns and contain no new information, will be filed with your recent records and will not receive a response.

If you have additional questions, Please call us at the toll-free number noted at the top of the first page. For your convenience, we are available 24 hours a day to assist you."

"If they're not going to respond to any of the really **important** questions, what kind of 'additional questions' do they think I'm really going to bother asking?", she mused.

* * *

Now that the dispute phase had been completed, Brooke was advised by the two members of the ADS Workgroup, Jen and Tom, that it was time for her to proceed immediately with the arbitration procedure.

"Don't give the banks any time to think or to act!", Tom told her. "Get those arbitrations under way ASAP". ADS seemed to be the Martin's only available life preserver in their rising sea of debt, so Brooke hastened to follow their every instruction.

She received a list of three small, independent arbitration associations that were recommended by ADS. One happened to be right in their own hometown. She was instructed to contact them directly via e-mail. Within 24 hours she received an e-mail response which included the proper forms to print out and submit, along with the requested $139.00 postal money order.

One cautionary statement surprised her however. She was told that the arbitration association which was located closest to her would be unable to arbitrate any dispute involving FunniBank.

Immediately, she telephoned the Workgroup to find out why. And for the first time since she had been dealing with ADS she found the Workgroup's telephone consistently on an answering machine.

After being unable to reach Jen or Tom for most of the day, Brooke resorted to emailing them. She asked why her local independent arbitration company was unable to arbitrate any cases involving FunniBank.

Anxiously, she checked her e-mail several times throughout that day and the next. Her stomach tightened and a general sense of uneasiness coursed through her each time she found no answer in her inbox.

By the third day she composed a second e-mail which reflected her sense of urgency and disappointment in the Workgroup's unavailability and lack of response.

Finally they wrote back. They indicated that FunniBank had sued her local independent arbitration company in order to prevent them from being qualified to impartially arbitrate any further cases involving FunniBank.

According to Tom, FunniBank had sued in order to tie up the arbitrators in court and harass them in retaliation for entering numerous arbitration awards in favor of its credit card customers and against FunniBank. The mere fact that FunniBank was suing them prevented the arbitration company from qualifying as unbiased arbiters.

Brooke was now beginning to sense the true scope of this battle.

Nothing that Albert had originally said to her indicated that any of the banks were making such an aggressive attempt to squelch this supposedly **legal** challenge to their money lending process. In fact, when he was selling her on the process, Albert made it sound like a piece of cake. "We have this list of questions that we present to the banks and they can't answer them so they just back off and close your credit card account and leave you alone!" he had assured her in that warm confident voice of his.

She really should have known better. It had *sounded* too good to be true and now a nagging whisper of doubt had situated itself in the back of her mind. Even if it is true that the banks make money out of nothing and just make unadulterated profit on these credit card accounts, how can we stand up against such   enormous and powerful institutions?!   But it seemed too late to turn back now.

Tom did gave her the name and e-mail address of another small, independent arbitration association located in the state of New York, and Brooke proceeded to make arrangements with them to deal with the FunniBank account. After setting all of these various wheels in motion, Brooke began to feel some sense of relief.

The small remains of their savings account had stopped dwindling month after month. These disputes *did* make sense to her. She was *not* just attempting to pull off some sort of bogus scheme in order to escape their debts... although the actual prospect of escape did feel like their last best hope - a desperate act born of necessity.

If she and her husband had not been convinced that the banks were doing something inherently dishonest and self-serving, they might have felt guilty for defaulting on four Credit Cards...but there was **so** much to lose, and what more could they lose by trying?

She buried any nagging doubts in the back of her mind, and awaited the results of the four arbitrations.

Hawley left it all up to her. It was all he could do to concentrate on his own demanding social work and bring home a paycheck with its associated health benefits. Their heads were now above water... or so it seemed.

Even though she consciously believed that she had it all under control, Brooke sometimes found herself standing in the middle of their living room in a sort of anxious daze. It came over her just as she was trying to catalog all of the various tasks that she needed to complete that particular day. That annoying hot flash sensation welled up and she broke into a nervous sweat.

"OK...ok... what is the most important thing that I need to get done first today? I should just make up my mind and do that... and then do the next most important thing."

She reached for a scratch pad and a pencil and started to jot down a "to do" list, and while she was doing that she felt afraid that she was forgetting something. The anxiety built, and she decided that the best thing for her to do right then was to exercise and alleviate this unbearable anxiety. After all, she knew that if she didn't make herself exercise she would be tempted to binge on corn chips or chocolate instead.

So she stepped shakily onto one of their exercise machines and worked herself up to a panting sweat. *"I'm too damned fat!"* She ruminated.

Later that evening while eating their dinner in front of the television set, Brooke saw another one of those informative diet pill commercials mentioning the so-called "stress hormone", cortisol.

A 3-D wire-frame diagram of a pudgy woman's body was slowly rotating in the center of the screen. It depicted a woman shaped just like Brooke. She carried 30lbs. of excess weight distributed primarily around her belly, hips and thighs.

"Stress..." she thought, *"...just like the commercial says. Should I call that 800 number and buy some of those pills? I wonder if they really work. But they must be expensive. How*

can I possibly justify spending any extra money to buy myself **diet pills** *for crissake?! I should just fuckin'* **eat less goddamn food** *and save money! Why am I such a* **fuckin' pig** *all the time?!"*

She did her best to put the brakes on this roller-coaster of self-loathing and told herself how intelligent she was and how she knew that with her capacity to comprehend such complicated information she should be quite capable of handling their case against any of these banks.

She had always been an achiever, and had always been able to prove to herself and others that she was exceptionally intelligent. This should be no different.

Maybe she *was* too fat, but she was also too damn smart to let this challenge defeat her. It seemed as if her entire self esteem was riding on this impending legal contest. She thought about what it would feel like to lose … what it would feel like to have their little remaining savings snatched out of their bank account… what it would feel like to see a Sheriff's cruiser pull into their driveway with a warrant to come into their home and seize their television set, their computers, their exercise equipment, her little bit of jewelry… and all because some old ultra-rich Federal Reserve bank with its special privilege to create money out of thin air wanted to get all of that **Vapor Money** back out of her and her husband.

She thanked goodness that they were living in a 100% homestead state like Florida. At least those filthy-rich counterfeiting loan sharks could not force them out of their home.

She leaned back on the couch in front of their television, snuggled against Hawley, and welcomed their beautiful 12-year-old kitty cat, Gabriel, to curl up into her lap. The gentle purring felt wonderful… and she gratefully stroked his soft fur. He gazed up at her so lovingly… so trustingly… and flexed his little paws with pleasure.

CHAPTER FOUR
Reeling

Brooke and Hawley took advantage of the lull which followed their submission of all four credit card accounts to "binding arbitration". Hawley went about his business as a social services professional, putting out the interpersonal fires which invariably flared up between displaced children and the foster parents who agreed to care for them for awhile.   Brooke became addicted to research – legal and otherwise. Diligently she explored the Internet looking for any conceivable reference material pertaining to the topic of "debt elimination".

In the course of this all-absorbing activity she came across the name "John Hagli". Interestingly enough, this John Hagli claimed to have pioneered the very process of debt elimination, and he insisted that ever since 1992 various greedy entities had plagiarized his materials. Brooke decided to follow up. She telephoned the ADS Workgroup. When Tom answered the phone, she spent a minute or two paving the road with pleasantries and then she got right to the point.

"Tom, what do you know about this guy John Hagli?" Pause. "Tom?"

"Uh… yeah. He used to work with us."

"Well he claims that he started this whole debt elimination idea. But he doesn't work with you guys anymore?"

"No. He can be rather difficult…", Tom offered, a cautious tone of voice becoming increasingly irrepressible. "He's really arrogant… and he just gets really… umm… hard to work with."

"He's got this website, and this long detailed blog where he names all these different people and companies that he says have plagiarized his copyrighted materials. And he names that guy Patrick who started ADS."

"Yeah... I know."

"He... he says that he's suing ADS."

"Yeah... I know."

"Well what do you think is going to happen? Is he going to put you out of business?"

"NO, no... He had a contract with us. He went into business with us. We have every right to use his materials. He's the one who copped out on us and left our company after he agreed to work with us."

"OH! Well, OK. But he says that your company is using out of date copies of all of those materials that he originated. He says that he is constantly improving and revising all his stuff and that all you guys are doing is selling people his old out of date stuff."

"Well, it's true that we haven't worked for him for about a year now, but we don't think he's really changed anything. We think he's just saying all that in order to take customers away from us now. I wouldn't worry about it, Brooke. We have our own staff of legal experts and paralegals who are keeping up with all of the latest tactics to use against these banks."

"Latest *tactics?* I thought this whole procedure was tried and **true**... and guaranteed to work as long as we followed your instructions to the letter."

"Oh yeah... you're absolutely right! And Patrick was just telling me that you are like this model customer who does everything exactly the way they're supposed to. There are so many other people who don't mail the dispute letters on time, or who expect us to do it all for them and they don't even understand what this is all about... so if *they* get sued they're not going to have a clue..."

"*Sued?!* We're not supposed to get **SUED!!!** This program is supposed to make the banks just zero out our credit card accounts and go way and leave us alone! We did the arbitration and **everything!**"

"Did you get your arbitration awards back yet?"

"No. I guess it's too soon, RIGHT?"

"How long ago did you submit your paperwork? Has it been a month?"

"No. It's been about fifteen days."

"Well just relax, Brooke. Wait 'till you get those four arbitration awards. You'll have plenty of ammunition in case they ever sue you."

"Ok. Well... I guess that's all the questions I have for now, Tom. Thanks for taking the time."

"Hey, no problem. You're one of our best customers."

"Uh-huh. Thanks. Bye for now."

"Bye."

Brooke felt shell-shocked. It was dawning on her that this was not such a "piece of cake" ... such a "walk in the park" ... such a predictably positive outcome.

We **didn't** have the all-powerful magic bullet that these companies seemed to describe on all their web sites. We were taking on "Goliath" and our slingshot just might be full of horseshit.

* * *

A couple of weeks later, right on schedule, the 'binding Arbitration Awards' arrived. Hawley was thrilled. They looked extremely official. The entire amount of each credit card debt was awarded to the Martins and the two or three members of each arbitration committee found against all four of the banks.

Brooke was very careful not to betray the nagging doubts that were rattling around in the back of her mind. Hawley had enough on his plate... he was earning a living for both of them. Brooke was trying to do her part by dealing with this unmanageable burden of debt.

She was both flattered and embarrassed by the praise that he lavished upon her for discovering this information and handling these disputes and producing these arbitration awards through her diligent efforts.

Several months went by and the two of them were almost giddy with relief. They even treated themselves to some new clothes and a few extra dinners out. But now they always made certain to pay off their one remaining credit union card every single month. They were grateful that the company had not closed out the account. After all, if anybody checked either of their credit reports now, they would find a certifiable disaster.

The only credit card they retained was the one associated with the credit union, and it carried no balance. They vowed never, ever to run up any credit card debts again.

Then one afternoon Hawley came home from work with a business card in his hand. The logo said "Sumter County Sheriff's Department", and the name "Deputy Brenda Foley" appeared underneath. There were a couple of blanks which she had filled in with today's date and the time she stopped by.

The Martins lived on several acres of forestland with a long driveway winding back through the trees. The entire property was fenced and the front gate was always locked. They had two big beautiful mongrel watchdogs appropriately named "Rolex" and "Timex" (the artist's sense of humor!). So Deputy Foley was forced to leave her card clipped to the chain link.

The Martins were barely able to see the driveway from the house, so unless they were expecting company and left the gates open, no one could enter the property without crashing the gate.

Brooke, especially, liked it that way. She was home alone so much of the time. In fact she felt so safe in their private park-like grounds that she spent most of her time at home only partially dressed. None of her neighbors could see a thing. This was Florida... balmy and beautiful in the winter... hot and steamy (punctuated by thunderstorms and hurricanes) in the summer. If you didn't **have** to wear clothes... you didn't.

It was obvious to both of them that this deputy Sheriff was trying to serve a summons. They delayed accepting it for as long as possible. They both wanted to gather their thoughts and gird themselves for the legal battle that was inevitably to come.

And right now they had to contend with an upcoming battle with mother nature. A hurricane named Francis was bearing down on Punta Gorda Florida, with its projected path going right through Sumter county.

Neither Brooke nor Hawley had ever lived through a hurricane. They had moved to Florida from southern California. Earthquakes they understood. Fires they had run from in years past. But hurricanes were an unknown quantity to both of them, and for that reason they probably reacted with more fear and more dread than any of the Florida natives who surrounded them.

Brooke's eldest brother, Bobby, was ready and willing to help her and her husband to prepare. He showed up in his truck with all of his power tools and helped them to board up their windows... cutting each of the pieces of plywood to fit while Hawley used his electric drill to make pilot holes in the window casements for the big masonry screws that would hold the plywood in place. "You've gotta protect these windows!", Bobby stressed. "If your windows blow out your roof might come off!" Brooke and Hawley just stood there in shock for a moment or two.

"We're so grateful for your help, brother Bob.", Hawley said softly as his brother-in-law packed all the tools back into the back of his truck.

"I'm so glad to do it.", he replied, with that warm Florida drawl. And they could tell he meant it. His T-shirt was soaked with sweat. He had come right on over to their house after boarding up all the windows at his own house and then at his office building. They were amazed that he had any stamina left to come to their house after doing all that. How could they ever repay him? What would they have done without him? They all hugged each other, caring nothing about their sweaty clothing or their sticky faces and hands. They were family.

Brooke and her husband locked the front gate after Bobby left and walked back to their house.

Hurriedly they cleaned up the residue of the window-boarding-up operation. They had been warned. Any material lying around in the yard could become a projectile and hurtle through a window... thereby causing the dreaded increase in air pressure within the house that could blow the roof right off. They were dirty and exhausted but they had to get this done.

The tops of the trees were beginning to swirl with the kind of motion that made Brooke feel seasick when she looked up. The usual happy cacophony of bird's song was suddenly absent. The two of them retreated into their now cave-like homestead.

They both knew that soon after the storm began, their electricity was bound to fail. So feeling dirty and desperate to get cleaned up before it was too late, they both scrambled into the shower. Their homestead was on a private well and it took electricity to power the water pump. As soon as the power went out there would be nothing but bottled water available to them and their four cats, two dogs and solitary horse. Every conceivable container had already been filled.

The big stockpot that Brooke used for soup or spaghetti sat filled with water on the shower floor. Next to it sat the turkey roasting pan, also filled to the brim and covered. Three plastic pitchers full of cool water took up the middle shelf in the refrigerator. Nine jugs full of bottled water from the grocery store sat just outside the back door. Their horse's great big water trough was filled to capacity outside. Brooke kept reassuring herself that she had thought of everything... done everything.

After their showers they stepped naked into the darkened living room and dried off in front of the television set.

The weather channel was broadcasting increasingly frightening radar images of the approaching storm. It had gathered strength and was now a category five hurricane bearing down on the southwest coast of Florida. All prognostications anticipated its landfall around Tampa and Saint Petersburg... then traversing north east across the state and right through Ocala on its way out to the Atlantic coast.

Suddenly it took an unexpected turn and slammed into Punta Gorda. No one there had really prepared. They all expected it to make land fall further north. The Martin's rural community of Oxford was right inside the cone of probability.

Again they agonized about whether or not they should pack up all the smaller pets in their little motor home and try to escape the path of the storm. But it kept on changing direction unexpectedly. They had no idea which way to go. Brooke felt like a panicked squirrel darting back and forth in front of an approaching vehicle, unable to make up its mind until it was too late. She couldn't bear to save herself and all the other pets, and desert her poor horse, Fleetwood.

Just as the news cameras finished broadcasting the devastation that befell Punta Gorda, and the storm was bearing down on Lake Wales in the heart of southern Florida, the Marten's power went out. The outer bands of the hurricane had already reached Oxford. It sounded like an endless freight train rushing by outside their boarded-up windows.

Already prepared with nine volt batteries and oversized flashlights, the Martins illuminated their living room just enough to get by. Four little pairs of eyes glistened from underneath the coffee table and behind the roll-top desk. Brooke and Hawley both knelt down and tried to comfort their frightened kitty cats. The two dogs were huddled inside their doghouse right next to the outside wall. Should they have put the dogs in crates and brought them inside? Would they be safer and happier in their doghouse, with freedom to move around?

There were just too many things to decide right now. They didn't know what was best any more. They paced back and forth, listening to the ferocious wind… wondering what it looked like outside.

Cautiously, Hawley cracked open the front door and they both peered out through the exterior storm door. They couldn't believe what was happening to their trees. The giant "granddaddy oaks" -- as all the local residents called them – appeared to be standing strong. Their trunks were six to 7ft. in diameter and rose 75 to 100 feet into the air.

It wasn't until the branches diminished to less than 1ft. in diameter that anything appeared to be moving. But when they did move they broke. The ground was littered with torn and broken branches. Each of these huge oaks was surrounded by a group of equally tall but much more slender trees like hickory, sweet gum, pecan, water oak, poplar and laurel. Those flexible trees performed a dizzying ballet as they alternated between bending completely over and swirling about in unpredictable, overlapping circles.

Each time one of them failed and broke with the strain, a sharp crack tore through the air and the ground shuddered as the limb slammed into the saturated soil below. The driveway was already completely blocked with debris. The wind began an intermittent, whistling howl that made the hair at the base of their necks stand on end. How much worse was this going to get?

Without the television and the weather channel they had no idea what path the storm was taking now. Hawley tracked down their portable radio and searched for the weather news. It wasn't hard to find. All of the local talk radio stations were concentrating on news of this hurricane. Tornado warnings had been issued for Sumter, Lake and Marion Counties. "Take shelter in an interior room with no windows..." the announcer stressed, "... or barricade yourselves behind furniture in an interior hallway." They looked at each other... each one seemingly waiting for the other to speak first. They both started at the same time.

"Let the cats into the linen closet, and barricade ourselves in the hallway!"

"OK!"

They had only one interior hall, and it was barely six feet long. It led to three doors: the second bathroom, and the second and third bedrooms. The open end of the hall led to the living room. As soon as the hall linen closet was opened, three out of four of their frightened cats scurried inside and huddled on the lower shelves. It was their favorite place to huddle during the usual Florida thunderstorms.

The other kitty had hunkered down behind a lamp table that fit between two large barrister bookshelves in the living room. That was her favorite hiding place.

Next, Brooke and Hawley dragged their behind-the-couch buffet table into the hallway, and centered it between the walls. Then they carried the heavy coffee table to the entrance of the hall, crawled in behind it together and turned it up on end. Together they crouched under the buffet table, behind the upright coffee table … praying that no tornado would tear their roof apart.

For several minutes the radio announcer tracked the progress of the funnel cloud as it ripped through the south end of their neighborhood. Then an eerie silence. One large 9-volt emergency flashlight sat on the kitchen counter and illuminated the living room. It cast harsh shadows among the displaced furniture. The one kitty, Dottie, who had hidden alone behind the lamp table in the living room, ventured out and cried for the rest of her family… a tentative, nervous little cry.

Thunderpuff, Gabriel and Sugarplum peeked out of the linen closet. That outer band of Hurricane Francis had apparently moved on. If that was only one of the *outer* bands, what must the *center* of the storm be like? They could not imagine.

Again they ventured to the front door, and cautiously peered outside. The scene out front was no comfort. Numerous broken branches blocked their driveway and littered the front lawn like twisted corpses on a battlefield. They hadn't realized that it was still pouring down rain. The boarded up windows had muffled the sound. Water rushed past the front door piling fallen leaves against the branches in its way.

"We can't move the cars!" Brooke whispered, as if whispering could make the situation any less threatening. "What if we need to go get something?"

"As soon as the rain lets up, we'll move those branches out of the way."

"But some of them are **huge!**"

"I know… I know… but we'll just have to do the best we can." He reached around her shoulders and pulled her close against him. "It's a good thing we started that video exercise program a few months ago!"

His warmhearted humor caught her off guard and she laughed. Then they heard the dogs barking. A Sheriff's deputy was parked outside their locked front gate. They knew that it was difficult to see the house clearly from the road, so they quietly stepped back inside and closed the door. "I don't *believe* it!" Brooke hissed… still whispering. "Why are they doing this *now*?"

"I dunno. Let's just give it a few more minutes… then we'll take another look." He checked his watch, and five minutes later they cracked open the front door. Sure enough, the deputy had pulled back out of their driveway and left something small and white clipped to the gate. Again the business card said: "Deputy Brenda Foley, Sumter County Sheriff's Department".

"Damn. How can we possibly respond to a summons right now? We have no electricity. I can't use my computer. I can't use my printer. We've just got to avoid this until we get our power back." Brooke felt the full weight of her responsibility to defend them against this lawsuit. After all, she was the one who found out all about this debt elimination scheme in the first place.

"It's OK Honey. It's not like they'll charge in here with guns drawn in order to serve us with a civil lawsuit about some stupid credit card debt. I think we can avoid this a while longer… at least until the electricity comes back on." Hawley was warm and reassuring as always. "Besides… we have all those arbitration awards."

"But how do we know how long we're going to be without power?"

"We don't. We'll just have to do the best we can. I can't stand being cooped up in here any longer. Let's get out there and see if we can move some of those branches out of the way."

"OK. Good idea. It'll keep my mind off all this crap for a while."

"Exactly!"

They changed into blue jeans and long sleeved shirts, even though the air was stifling outside, grabbed a spray can of "Deep Woods Off" ®, and ventured forth. First Hawley stood with his arms outstretched while Brooke sprayed his clothes with mosquito repellent. Then he returned the favor.

They stepped over a variety of fallen branches to get to their storage shed and fetched their two pair of leather work gloves. Then they turned and looked at the enormous mess which awaited them. No electricity. They could not use their electric chain saw.

Within two minutes the salty grubby sweat was trickling down their foreheads and burning their eyes. It took both of them working together to lift most of the larger fallen branches and set them to the side of the circular driveway. The once pretty lawn that Brooke had taken such pains to cultivate was now cluttered with a sprawling gnarly heap of broken limbs. It would be months before she saw that lawn again.

* * *

Back inside the house, they peeled off their sodden, stinking, sweat soaked clothing. Both of them wanted a shower. But there was no power... nothing to run their electric well pump. They could not flush the toilets or fill a glass of tap water.

Brooke fetched a jug from the emergency stores on the back porch and they stood in the darkened kitchen passing the water back and forth between them. The radio sputtered in the background, broadcasting the latest escapades of Hurricane Francis. "We got done just in time!" Hawley exclaimed. "Listen... it's raining again."

"There's our shower!" Brooke bubbled, and headed for the door. Then, forgetting something, she darted back to the bathroom and grabbed the soap dish. He caught on fast and followed her outside. Together they stood under the waterfall which always formed in the valley of their "L-shaped" roof whenever it rained. The property was so private that they didn't worry a minute about exposing themselves to the neighbors. This was survival! They washed and shampooed and peed outside together in the tropical downpour.

"well! At least we won't have to worry about flushing the toilets for a while!", they laughed.

It took about fifteen minutes for them both to start feeling sticky, sweaty, and uncomfortable again. Without air conditioning their boarded up homestead became a damp and musty cave. And this was only the first day.

It took a week for the emergency electrical crews who came from all over the United States to restore their power. By that time mold had begun growing on the ceiling in the master bathroom, and under the kitchen sink. Everything in their refrigerator spoiled. They dragged three Hefty bags full of rotting food out of the house, and squatted over plastic supermarket bags when they had to have a bowel movement. They continued to slip outside when they needed to urinate.

Fortunately they had the foresight to stock up on canned foods and prepackaged snacks. They had plenty of cat food and dog food and hay for their horse. The torrential rains continued to refill Fleetwood's ample water trough.

Whenever their masters slipped outside to use nature's bathroom, the two affectionate watch dogs clamored for attention. It was both awkward and funny to be eliminating in the underbrush while two dogs were avidly attempting to push their noses in unwanted places.

The only convenience which still functioned was the hard wired telephone. Hawley called in to work the first business day after the hurricane and explained that there were still too many large fallen branches blocking their driveway for him to be able to leave the property.

Two days later they had managed to clear the driveway and the man of the house left for work wearing damp and rumpled clothing.

While he was there that day attempting to make sense of his disrupted case load of foster families, Sheriff's deputy Brenda Foley appeared at his place of employment. There, in front of his mystified colleagues, the respected social worker was served with a Summons and Complaint.

CHAPTER FIVE
On the Hook

As soon as he had a moment to himself, Hawley picked up the cell phone and called home.

"The Sheriff's deputy showed up at my place of employ today." he offered.

"They served you with a court case?"

"That's what it looks like."

"Do you want to open it and read to me?"

"No... let's just wait until I get home OK?"

"Sure, Honey, that's fine." she acquiesced. But Brooke really wished that he had been willing to tear it open right then and there and read it aloud to her. That way she wouldn't have to wonder what in the heck it was all afternoon. Not enough distraction existed to keep her mind off of that complaint until her husband returned home. The hours passed slowly for her.

Hawley had so much to deal with at work that the rest of the day seemed to evaporate. He was headed out to the parking lot before he had another thought about the summons and complaint. "Those arbitration awards were supposed to have taken care of all this." he muttered to himself.

Mercifully, his colleagues had gone about their business without pressing him with nosy questions all afternoon. He set the eight-and-a-half by eleven manila envelope on the passenger seat. It remained unopened until he walked into the living room and handed it to Brooke. She will handle it, he thought. He counted on her.

Immediately she hurried over to the desk and pulled out the letter opener. The stack of papers inside was about 3/8 inch thick.

The first page consisted of the summons:

"A lawsuit has been filed against you. You have twenty calendar days after this summons is served on you to file a written response to the attached Complaint in this court."

"A phone call will not protect you; you're written response, including the above case number and named parties, must be filed if you want the court to hear your case. If you do not file your response on time, you may lose the case, and your wages, money, and property may thereafter be taken without further warning from the court. There are other legal requirements. You may want to call an attorney right away. If you do not know an attorney, you may call an attorney referral service or a legal aid office (listed in the phone book)."

"If you choose to file a written response yourself, at the same time you file your written response to the Court you must also mail or take a carbon copy or photocopy of your written response to:

Plaintiff's Attorney,

Pat Answers, Esquire,

P.O. Box 74332,

Orlando, FL 32857-4332."

The following paragraph included information which would have been important if Hawley had been disabled. On the next page was the complete complaint:

COMPLAINT

"Plaintiff sues Defendant and alleges:

1. This is an action for damages in the amount of $_____.

2. Defendant made or authorized certain purchases of goods and/or services from various vendors using a credit card.

3. Those purchases were charged to the associated credit card account XXXX XXXX XXXX XXXX; the account is owned by plaintiff.

4. The applicable vendors were paid by Plaintiff for the purchases made by Defendant, and in turn the Plaintiff sent billing statements to Defendant seeking reimbursement for those payments; a copy of the final statement showing the balance due is attached.

5. Defendant has not fully paid the balance due on the credit card account, said balance being comprised of purchases made by Defendant, less payments and credits, plus interest, service charges and fees.

6. Defendant owes Plaintiff $_____., which is the balance due on the account.

WHEREFORE, Plaintiff demands judgment against the Defendant in the sum of $_____, together with costs, interest, and such other relief as the court may deem just and proper. This is a communication from a debt collector.

Pat Answers, P.A.

Defendant's copy"

The balance of this very thick bundle of paperwork was comprised of monthly statements from FunniBank going back over the last two years. They all appeared to be Xerox copies – often crooked on the page. Some Secretary had slapped them one by one onto the copy machine, and had not been particularly neat about it.

About four pages from the end was the monthly billing statement showing a credit for the **$20.00** which had been the **"Notice of Final Payment and Agreement to Arbitrate"** check.

More proof that FunniBank had accepted it and cashed it. Now Brooke had to figure out the best way to respond.

I'm supposed to be able to rely on the ADS workgroup, she reminded herself. I'll e-mail them right now.

She took the Complaint and scanned it; then attached it to an e-mail addressed to:

workgroup@nobk.com. In her e-mail, Brooke informed the workgroup that her husband had been sued by FunniBank. Naturally, she asked them to let her know what she should do next and how to do it.

Two days went by – no answer.

She sent a second e-mail, containing more urgent language and complaining that they only had twenty days in which to respond before they could lose by default. Four days had elapsed already. The following day she received her reply.

The so called workgroup was no longer available for free to customers who had been sued. They were now providing a new level of service which was to be known as: "Summons Support", and it would be billed on a separate basis… in addition to the $2,500.00 they had already paid for the ADS Debt Elimination Program.

Shaking, Brooke picked up the phone and dialed the ADS office in Southern Florida. "Hello… this is Brooke Martin, one of your Debt Elimination customers? I need to speak to Albert please."

"I'm sorry, Albert is no longer with us."

"What happened to him?"

"He's become ill… he had to quit."

"Well I need to talk to one of the owners… one of the people in charge."

"OK. I'll connect you with Patrick." About 30 seconds later, a male voice addressed her.

"Hello, this is Patrick. May I help you?"

"Yes… I hope so. This is Brooke Martin; I'm one of your customers. We're being sued."

"Did you follow our letter writing program exactly as instructed?"

"Yes, I certainly did."

"Did you proceed to arbitration?"

"Yes. And we received four arbitration awards in our favor. But now one of the banks is suing us."

"Which one? Is it FunniBank?"

"Yeah! How did you know?"

"They're suing **everybody** now."

"**WHAT?!** Albert told me that following your program would make these banks just give up and go away with their tails between their legs."

"It used to. But a couple of these banks are playing hardball now. We've gotten under their skin."

"Wait a minute! Albert made me think that this was a tried and true program that would legally enable me to eliminate these credit card debts!"

"We promised to get you the arbitration awards, and we **did** get you the arbitration awards."

"But what good are they if we're just going to get sued *anyway?!*"

"You can get the arbitration awards confirmed by the court and then even if one of the banks does sue you, you can use the arbitration award as a defense."

"Hold it! *Nobody* told me that you still had to get the arbitration awards confirmed by a court! I thought the whole point was to stay **out** of court, and that the arbitration forum would have a more consumer friendly outlook!"

"They **do**. Most of the time the banks just give up after they lose in arbitration. FunniBank is the most aggressive. They've started suing **everybody**. When the situation changes, we **all** have to adapt."

"You gave me a money back guarantee. If my debt doesn't get eliminated, I'm supposed to get my money back."

"We promised you that you'd get an arbitration award in your favor if you followed the program exactly as we instructed you. You did that and now you have your arbitration awards. If anything else happens we have to charge you for the time that it takes the workgroup to help you fight a court case."

"So how much is *that* going to be now?"

"About $3,000.00."

"**Are you *kidding* me?** That's **more** than we paid in the ***first*** place! **You people are a fucking *rip off!*"**

"I'm sorry you feel that way ma'am. If you need our help with the lawsuit please call back and we'll make arrangements for you to use our Summons Support Program." Brooke said nothing further. She simply hung up the telephone.

"*SH_H_H_I_T!!!*" she hissed aloud to herself.

Immediately she called her brother Bobby. He was constantly engaging in a variety of legal battles and representing himself pro se. He promptly recommended a man whom he considered to be an intelligent and experienced paralegal. A man named Jeff. Bobby offered to drive his sister over to Jeff's house the next day so that she could begin to work with him on this case.

That new plan caused the nervous tension to drain out of Brooke's body so suddenly that she nearly sank to the floor. Bracing herself against the refrigerator, she opened the right hand side and reached in to grab herself a light beer. Being only an occasional drinker, and having had very little to eat that afternoon, she managed to slip into a contented fog until bed time. Hawley heated something up in the microwave for dinner.

* * *

Brooke awakened the next morning emotionally prepared to do battle. Bobby met her at his office and drove her out to meet Jeff.

As they pulled up to his home, Brooke wondered why a respected paralegal would be living like a Florida 'cracker'. The house was old, and appeared to be one of those 'add-on' projects. Various materials covered different sections of the building and the damp grass was over a foot long. Before they could step out of the car, a large dog appeared and barked aggressively.

Unafraid, Bobby opened the driver's side door and stepped out. Brooke remained in the passenger seat while

Bobby knocked on the nearest door. It appeared to open into a makeshift 'Florida room' – a screen-enclosed porch.

After a minute or two, Jeff appeared. He greeted Bobby and noticed Brooke holed-up in the car. Smiling and barefoot, he stepped outside and told his dog to lie down. Reassured, Brooke ventured out onto the shaggy lawn. She wondered how anyone could dare to walk barefoot in such deep grass... grass that could conceal a multitude of creatures which she would not want in contact with her bare feet.

Once she and her big brother had been escorted into the house, she had a chance to relax and appreciate Jeff's appearance. Handsome, she thought... as handsome as a movie star.

When he first extended his hand to her in greeting, and her eyes quickly traveled the length of this form, she was actually startled. She thought she might have noticed him recognizing that fact, when a little knowing grin materialized on his well-formed lips. A combination of Michael Landon and Hugh O'Brien, she thought. So why was he alone?

Maybe it was the curse of beauty. Maybe because women just came onto him for his looks, and never took the time to get to know the man. Or maybe because he knew it all too well and remained single just to play the field. Brooke was leery of men who were *too* attractive... and then she realized that it was the 'curse of beauty' in action, right there, in her own mind. At that point, she felt a certain sympathy for him. Someone should appreciate him for himself, she thought. I wonder how bright he is?

They all settled in the eclectic and cluttered living area adjacent to the neglected looking kitchen. Jeff sat near her on the brown leather couch. Macho furniture, she mused. After a few pleasantries, he began asking questions about their case, and she pulled out the Complaint. He rummaged among some objects on the end table, and found his department store reading glasses. Everyone remained quiet while he scanned it.

"I think we should file a Motion for More Definite Statement.", he announced. "Look at this Complaint. The attorney didn't even sign it. And notice at the bottom where it says, 'This is a communication from a debt collector.' We can't be sure if this attorney really represents FunniBank or whether he is actually an attorney that purchased the debt and is acting on his own behalf."

Brooke had a general idea of what Jeff was getting at. She had been poking around on the Internet and found a few bulletin boards on which credit card debtors were discussing their cases.

One of the issues they were raising concerned so-called third party debt collectors. Some of the debt elimination web sites mentioned that debtors could escape paying third party debt collectors because the debtor never actually signed a contract with any third party. Without a signed contract the debt collector was supposedly unable to obtain a judgment.

But the debtor had to know exactly how to defend himself, and how to assert the issue correctly, or the bank's attorneys would ride roughshod over him.

Brooke was pleased to hear Jeff allude to this issue. Obviously he knew what he was doing. She heaved a quiet sigh, and her stomach muscles relaxed. The Easter-egg-sized knot next to her left shoulder blade still gave her an occasional twinge, however.

"Do you need a retainer, Jeff?"

"I usually ask for $500.00 up front.", he offered. Brooke visibly blanched. "But because I've done so much business with your brother Bobby… $200.00 today would be fine."

Brooke pulled two $100.00 bills out of her wallet and graciously handed them to Jeff. He tossed them casually onto the coffee table. This rather indifferent gesture surprised her. Jeff seemed to have the cultivated air of a mature Huckleberry Finn: barefoot, devil-may-care; iconoclastic.

She did realize that he must have been helping her older brother with his notorious tax protest activities.

Although certainly not mainstream, many of these guys had a real command of the law; especially Constitutional law. She definitely needed moral, intellectual, and legal support in this upcoming contest.

They exchanged e-mail addresses, and Brooke left Jeff a thick folder containing copies of all the debt elimination materials she had purchased from Alternative Debt Services; including the series of dispute letters she had been instructed to mail to all four of the banks.

* * *

Back at the house, Brooke and Hawley continued to cope with the power outage that Hurricane Francis had visited upon them. How in the world could she receive an e-mail from Jeff, and print out the legal documents that he would prepare for them when they had no electricity and could not operate either their computer or printer?

A few months ago they had purchased a 6250 watt generator on sale for $450.00. They knew it was a bargain, and they knew that one day a generator might become a necessity. But they had no idea how to set it up to provide power to the entire house. Again, her brother Bobby came to the rescue.

Brooke and Hawley followed Bobby's instructions and located the generator near the outside of their house next to the electric meter. Bobby took Brooke with him to the nearest hardware store and selected the appropriate wire and special plug.

As the couple watched, Bobby attached the four separate wires that were encased inside the large wire to their appropriate contacts inside the plug. One black wire and one red wire would supply power to the house, and one white wire was neutral while the copper wire would be the ground.

Next, Bobby removed the electric power meter and fed the four loose ends of the wire through the wall next to the wires which already led from the power meter to the breaker box inside the house. Despite the fact that no power was coming from the city power company at the time, Bobby still turned the main breaker to the "off" position before doing any of this work. Then he detached the two city power supply wires from the breaker switch that supplied power to the electric range. Patiently he showed Brooke and her husband how to attach the two power wires from the generator – black and red – to the two contacts which normally supplied power to the range.

"The generator can't supply enough power to run your electric oven, so you can't use it anyway. So we're going to bring the power from the generator in through that breaker."

"How much of the stuff inside the house will the generator be able to run?" Hawley asked.

"Basically just the lights, the television or the computer, and the refrigerator… and the water pump from your well. Don't try to run too many things at once."

"No air conditioning?"

"Nope. It don't begin to have enough power to run the air conditioning. It can't run your hot water heater either, but it will run your water pump. Even though you've got to take cold showers for a while you're going to be glad just to have the fresh well water and be able to take a shower."

"That's for sure!" As soon as Bobby finished wiring everything up, Hawley tried to start up the generator. It sputtered and died.

"Did ya open up the fuel supply line?" Bobby asked.

"I don't know what you mean." (Hawley was a wonderful social worker but he knew absolutely nothing about most mechanical devices).

"Lemme take a look." Bobby bent down next to the generator and looked underneath the fuel tank. "Here it is… right here. You've got to open up this little valve and let the gasoline flow down into the motor!"

"OH…OK!" Brooke piped in. As soon as the valve was opened Bobby yanked the pull chord and started the engine right up. The generator sounded like an extra loud lawn mower. She opened the side door and saw that the overhead light in their little office room had come on. Then she darted through the office and looked into the living room – LIGHTS! Hallelujah! And the ceiling fans were running! She heard the refrigerator start back up, too. "It's working!!!"

"OH GOD! We are SO grateful to you for helping us with this Bobby!", Hawley exclaimed.

"I'm so glad to do it.", he humbly replied, looking down into the back of his truck as he packed up his tools. They all hugged each other and said "Goodbye".

Bobby and his wife had been living in their motor home parked next to their house ever since the power went out. It had been almost a week now. Because they had the motor home to live in Bobby and Carol didn't bother with a generator for their house.

* * *

About three days later, Brooke checked her e-mail and Jeff came through with his <u>Motion for More Definite statement</u>::

DEFENDANT'S MOTION FOR MORE DEFINITE STATEMENT

COMES NOW the Defendant, Hawley V. Martin, to move this Honorable Court pursuant to Florida Rule of Civil Procedure 1.140(e) to order a more definite statement from the Plaintiff.

It is unclear from the papers served upon the Defendant as to whom the Plaintiff really is in this action. The alleged complaint served upon the Defendant Lists FunniBank as the Plaintiff, the last paragraph alleges that the action is a communication from a debt collector, yet the alleged complaint (Exhibit 1) served upon the Defendant is not signed as "Counsel for Plaintiff." In point of fact, the document served upon the Defendant is unsigned. In the space for a signature, under "PAT ANSWERS, P.A." is the typed notation "Defendant's copy."

The Defendant moves the Court to order clarification as to whether the attorney whose name appears typed is suing as counsel on behalf of FunniBank, or on his own behalf as collecting for himself and his firm. This clarification goes toward the establishment of jurisdiction and standing to sue, or lack thereof."

Brooke was impressed. The phraseology was professional and right to the point. Best of all, Jeff had sent it to her attached to an e-mail message. How convenient! How high-tech! She copied the file to her hard drive under the heading: "FunniBank Case", then opened it in Microsoft Word and printed it out. It looked terrific. Then she remembered that she needed three copies and printed out the other two.

Next, she prepared the envelope for the plaintiff's attorney. When Hawley returned home from work she presented him with all three copies for his signature. He was equally impressed. Next morning, she mailed the one copy to the attorney in Orlando and drove the second copy right to the downtown County Courthouse.

This was her first time at the courthouse since she had performed jury duty two years earlier. She knew right where to park. She walked into the building carrying nothing but her car keys and the folder containing the legal documents: one copy for the court and the other copy to be stamped by the court clerk and retained for her own files. She approached the security checkpoint just inside the main entrance and dutifully dropped her car keys into the wicker basket before walking through the metal detector. Then an authoritative male voice stopped her in her tracks.

"Excuse me Ma'm. You cannot bring this keychain into the courthouse." Surprised, she turned and faced a rather corpulent security guard. "This keychain has a pocket knife on it. No knives allowed in the courthouse!"

"OH! Can't you just keep it here for me? I'll be right back… I just have to…"

"No, Ma'm. No knives allowed in the courthouse at all. I'm sorry."

"That's OK. I understand. I'll go back and leave it in the car." Obediently, she took her keys from the man's chubby hand and walked back out to her car. She opened the driver's side door, nervously removed her pocket knife from the keychain, locked the car again, and took only the keys back to the courthouse with her. She would remember this next time. She certainly did not want to attract any undue attention... or be considered any kind of a problem whatsoever.

She smiled at the security guard as she handed him her car keys sans pocket knife. She thought he might acknowledge her spirit of cooperation with a responsive nod or at least a little grin... but no. His indifference stung her little bit, but she stepped on into the courthouse lobby with a feeling of determination. Now she had to figure out where the circuit court clerk's office was. A nicely dressed man with a briefcase walked briskly toward the courthouse entrance. He was obviously on his way out. "Excuse ... excuse me sir..." and he paused, "... would you please tell me where the circuit court clerk's office is?"

"Civil or criminal?"

"Uh...um...**Civil!**"

"Up the stairs; past the elevators; right turn; first door to your left."

"Thanks!" he made a minimal and polite gesture acknowledging her 'thanks' and continued on his way to the parking lot. He must be a person who prefers the stairs to the elevator, she mused with a smile... just like me! So up the stairs she marched, noticing the truly beautiful architecture of this modern day courthouse. The entire front of the building consisted of three stories worth of windows held in place with as few reinforcements as possible. Daylight illuminated the entire lobby. Quite elegant. She found the clerk's office exactly as instructed and walked up to the counter. Two pleasant looking ladies occupied a pair of desks behind it. One of them approached the counter. "May I help you?"

"Yes. I'd like to file this motion and keep the second copy for our records."

"Is this the correct court for you?" Obviously this clerk had never seen Brooke before and was more accustomed to seeing strangers walk into the wrong offices.

"Yes, I think so." Brooke placed the documents on the counter and the lady looked them over. The clerk appeared surprised.

"OK... just a moment." The clerk stamped each copy with the name of the circuit court, today's date... and the word "copy" on the second one, handing it back to Brooke. *"I obviously don't look like the usual lawyer or paralegal who walks into this office",* she thought. *"They probably expected me to be looking for the small claims court."* She chuckled softly, glancing down at her own faded blue jeans and sandals.

Feeling determined and proactive she marched back to her car, cranked up the radio on the oldies channel and drove home listening to The Rolling Stones, The Doors, and The Mama's And The Papas - all songs that tended to make her exceed the speed limit. She kept one eye on the rear view mirror... but here in rural Florida she hardly ever saw a police car. Most of the time she traveled between 60 and 75 miles per hour on these long, straight, two-lane back-country roads.

CHAPTER SIX

Breaking the Line

Brooke arrived back home in a pretty good mood. Taking positive action had always gratified her – all her life. The refusal to knuckle under to domineering people, and such defiance of authority were intrinsic to her nature. In fact, even reliance upon her helpful paralegal made Brooke uneasy. *"How do I know if he's taking the best approach? I can't evaluate his work if I don't take steps to educate myself!"* she thought. So she sat down at her computer and surfed the net for any possible information concerning the **pro se** conduct of legal matters. *"Besides… If I can learn to do some of this myself I can save some of the money we're having to spend on the paralegal."*

It didn't take long for her to happen upon just the right webpage: www.jurisdictionary.com. There she found materials that were guaranteed to de-mystify the legal process and were supposed to enable her to conduct either a legal offense **or** defense all by herself. The tab was a mere $220.00… so she ordered this tutorial immediately.

As soon as her payment cleared, the materials were available for download. Within minutes, Brooke was poring over several detailed Adobe ® .pdf documents and an animated tutorial all about how to file pre-trial motions, conduct discovery, file requests for production of documents, and answer a Complaint, among other things.

She found it all to be intelligently presented and quite easy to understand. The Florida attorney who had formulated these materials kept stressing his point that most anyone could learn to handle their legal problems without having to hire an attorney. She could hardly believe her good fortune in finding this website. "Thank GOODNESS for the Internet!!!" she said aloud.

Brooke was especially thrilled to learn how to comprehend the process of filing pre-trial motions. Jurisdictionary called it the "flurry of motions", and although her paralegal had prepared their pre-trial Motion for More Definite Statement for them correctly, Brook really hadn't understood its purpose… or that this sort of motion was something which had to be answered by the opposition before she and Hawley would even have to answer the Complaint itself.

Apparently, the Plaintiff could not proceed with the actual case until any and all such pre-trial motions had been dealt with by the Court. Jurisdictionary explained that there were numerous such motions which might be appropriate, and explained exactly how and why to prepare them.

This felt empowering and exciting. Brooke stayed up late into the night studying, marveling at, and absorbing this information. The following day she was bleary-eyed and nearly exhausted, but she felt that she would finally be able to comprehend the legal process and anticipate the correct way to respond to their adversaries.

* * *

The Martins' computer didn't demand much electricity, and the generator that her brother Bobby helped them to set up chugged away outside as she remained glued to the monitor for days. It took a full week for the local power company to restore their electricity, but thanks to that generator, Brooke was able to study and absorb her new legal tutorials.

About this time, an envelope from the Judge arrived. Inside, Brooke found the following:

ORDER TO RESPOND AND
MOTION PRACTICE ORDER

THIS CAUSE comes before the Court on Defendant's Motion for More Definite Statement, filed XXXXXXX XX 200X. After reviewing the file, it is hereby:

ORDERED: Plaintiff, upon receipt of this Order, shall have ten (10) calendar days to respond to Defendant's Motion. It is further,

ORDERED: to facilitate an orderly progression of this cause and better informed decisions by the Court, all future motions shall be handled in the following manner:

1) Legal memorandum required. In making any written motion or other application to the Court for the entry of an order of any kind, the moving party shall file and serve with such motion or application a legal memorandum with citations to authority in support of the relief requested. A supporting memorandum may be incorporated into the body of the motion but should be clearly titled, "Motion to/for --------------- and Memorandum of Law."

The following motions need not be accompanied by a memorandum of law:

A. Motion for continuance;

B. Motion for default addressed to the Court;

C. Motion for confirmation of sale;

D. Motion to withdraw or substitute exhibits;

E. Motion to proceed informa pauperis;

F. Motion for extension of time in which to complete discovery (providing good cause is set forth in the motion); and

G. Motion to withdraw or substitute counsel.

2) Timely opposing memoranda. Each party opposing any written motion or other application shall file and serve, within ten (10) calendar days after being served with such motion or application, a legal memorandum with citations to authority in opposition to the relief requested. Failure to respond within the time allowed may be deemed sufficient cause for granting the motion by default. If a party has no objection to a motion and does not intend to file a responsive memorandum, counsel shall file a written notice with the clerk of the Court so indicating.

3) Replies. If upon receipt of an opposing memorandum, counsel determines further argument of his client's position is required, s/he may notify the Court or the Courts law clerk in

writing that s/he intends to file and serve a reply memoranda. In such case, determination of the matter will be deferred by the Court for up to five (5) days pending preparation and filing of the reply.

4) Discovery motions accompanied by good faith certification. Before filing a motion to compel pursuant to the Florida Rules of Civil Procedure, Rule 1.380, or a motion for protective order pursuant to Rule 1.280 (c), counsel shall confer with counsel for the opposing party in a good faith effort to resolve by agreement the issues raised, and shall certify to the Court at the time of filing the motion that s/he has conferred with opposing counsel and has been unable to resolve the dispute.

5) Content of discovery motions. Except for motions grounded upon a complete failure to respond to discovery, discovery motions shall: (1) quote in full each interrogatory, question on deposition, request for an admission, or request for production to which the motion is addressed; (2) quote in full the objection and grounds given therefore; (3) state (with citations to authority) the reasons such objection should be overruled or sustained.

(6) Oral argument. Motions and other applications will ordinarily be determined by the Court on the basis of motion papers and legal memoranda unless a hearing is required by rule or law. (For example, under the rules, summary judgment motions should be set for hearing. This would not, however, extinguish the requirement that the motion be accompanied by and responded to with memoranda.)

The Court may permit oral argument upon the written request of any interested party or upon the Court's own motion. Requests for oral argument must accompany the motion or opposing legal memorandum and must estimate the time required for argument. When a request for hearing is granted, counsel for the requesting party will be asked to coordinate the calendars of the Court and counsel.

7) Page limitation. Absent prior permission of the Court, no party shall file a legal memorandum in excess of fifteen (15) pages in length.

8) Motions to be filed with the Clerk. All original pleadings and papers shall be filed with the Clerk of the Court.

9) Form of motions. All applications to the Court requesting relief in any form, or citing authorities or presenting argument with respect to any matter awaiting decision, shall be made in writing in accordance with this order and in appropriate form pursuant to the Florida rules of civil procedure, and unless invited or directed by the Court, shall not be addressed or presented to the Court in the form of a letter or the like.

10) Time calculations. All time calculations herein shall be subject to Rule 1.090, Florida Rules of Civil Procedure.

11) In Limine motions. In Limine motions will be heard at the pre trial conference.

12) Emergency motions. Motions of an emergency nature may be considered and determined by the Court at any time in its discretion.

Failure of either party to comply with the terms of this order may result in the striking of pleadings or parts of them or staying further proceedings until this order is obeyed or dismissing the action or rendering judgment by default against the disobedient party.

It occurred to Brooke that this Order was intended to discourage anyone from handling their own case Pro Se... but in the end, she used it to her own advantage... as we shall see.

The Plaintiff's Response was served on them by mail a week or so later. It answered their Motion for More Definite Statement as follows:

"RESPONSE TO MOTION FOR MORE DEFINITE STATEMENT"

"COMES NOW the Plaintiff, by and through undersigned council, and files this RESPONSE TO MOTION FOR MORE DEFINITE STATEMENT:

1. The style of the case clearly reflects that the Plaintiff is FunniBank (South Dakota), N.A., the issuer of the "Funni Platinum Select" credit card, as shown on the credit card statements filed with the complaint.

2. There is no requirement under the law that the Defendant's copy of the complaint be signed by the Plaintiff or attorney for Plaintiff.

3. The phrase "this is a communication from a debt collector" (or a similar phrase) is required to be included in all "communications" to debtors from third party debt collectors by the Fair Debt Collection Practices Act; while the Act excludes "pleadings" from this requirement, the undersigned, as a third party debt collector, includes the language in every communication he has with debtors as a precautionary practice."

Brooke realized what her paralegal had been trying to accomplish. Their Motion For More Definite Statement was intended to reveal whether or not this attorney was the actual current owner of this debt, rather than just a legal representative of this Plaintiff.

During her research she had come across a couple of essays describing this particular subterfuge. Some attorneys would apparently contract with the banks to retain the right to sue on behalf of the original lender... as if they were still just representing the bank, when they'd already purchased the debt for themselves.

This was intended to prevent Defendants from asserting that they had no contract with the debt collecting attorneys. But according to this response, the plaintiff was indeed FunniBank.

The City electrical power had been restored, the air conditioner was up and running, and now, in relative comfort, Brooke pondered what should be done next. Now she knew that it would be the second in a possible "flurry of motions" – all done in an effort to have this case dismissed without ever having to answer the Complaint.

Until studying her Jurisdictionary materials, Brooke had no idea that anyone could forestall answering the Complaint in any way whatsoever. Jeff had never offered to explain this to her... and in her former ignorance, she'd had no idea what questions to ask him... but she did understand that he was not motivated to teach himself out of a job.

Buoyed by her increasing knowledge and her own creative intelligence, she decided to focus now upon the issue of jurisdiction... and she wondered if she could do so without relying upon the paralegal.

According to the rules of civil procedure, an agreement to arbitrate constitutes a waiver of the right to sue in court. This **should** mean that the plaintiff could not obtain jurisdiction to sue.

So Brooke retrieved the original arbitration agreement letter that she had sent to FunniBank, her bank statement indicating the debit after they cashed her $20.00 check, and a printout of the canceled check.

Reluctant to step into the fray alone just yet, she telephoned Jeff to discuss their strategy. He already had copies of everything, and his opinions concerning the best way to proceed impressed her. So she hired him to prepare the next pleading too – he had already put so much thought into it. Within two days he emailed her this well-written:

DEFENDANT'S MOTION TO DISMISS AND MEMORANDUM OF LAW

COMES NOW the Defendant, Hawley Martin, to move this Honorable Court to dismiss that action for lack of jurisdiction pursuant to the terms of the agreement between the Plaintiff and the Defendant.

As evidence of the lack of jurisdiction of this Honorable Court the Defendant would place into evidence Exhibit 1. Exhibit 1 is a letter written by the Defendant on March 25, 2004, which, amongst other things, included a tender of final payment (satisfaction and accord), the cashing of which consented to explicit acceptance of binding arbitration, and a waiver of the right to bring this action:

"You also agree, by accepting this final payment, to binding arbitration in a forum of our choice which is not the American Arbitration Association or the National Arbitration Forum, for the purpose of resolving the existing dispute identified in this notice and any other dispute we may send, Your acceptance of my final payment and agreement to binding arbitration waives your right to maintain any lawsuit against us in any court."

Page two of Exhibit 1 demonstrates that the check was cashed, the terms accepted. By such agreement this Honorable Court is denied jurisdiction to hear this cause. Coggin Automotive Corp. v. Reed, 750 So. 2d 744 (5 DCA 2000).

On May 20, 2004, the _____ Arbitrations Corporation, successor in interests to _____ Corporation, granted an award in the binding arbitration of this issue to the Defendants in this action. Exhibit 2.

Under Florida law, as Roe correctly notes, arbitration is a favored means of dispute resolution and courts indulge every reasonable presumption to uphold proceedings resulting in an award. Beach Resorts Int'l, Inc. v. Clarmac Marine Constr. Co., 339 So.2d 689, 690 (Fla. 2d DCA 1976). Roe v. Amica Mutual Insurance Co., 533 S. 2d 279 (Fla. 1988).

CONCLUSION

FunniBank was given actual notice at all times and at all phases of the dispute, arbitration and of the award. FunniBank did not raise any objections to the venue of the arbitration, and accepted the waiver of judicial review of the outcome of the binding arbitration into which it entered. As the courts have pointed out in *Amica* (supra) this Honorable Court should uphold the proceeding, the resultant award, and FunniBank's waiver of suit if it did not like the outcome of the arbitration.

This action should be dismissed for lack of jurisdiction in that FunniBank has no standing to bring this action having waived such right.

Hawley was impressed and relieved. He read it and he signed it... grateful that Jeff and his wife had the time and the acumen to learn how to deal with this. First thing next day, she filed their Motion with the Clerk of the Court.

Brooke plunged into this new realm of knowledge with enthusiasm. She needed to feel useful and capable... and above all, she needed to make up for no longer bringing in the top-notch salary that she used to command.

She didn't consciously recognize the fact that her entire bubble of self-esteem seemed to collapse with the loss of her position as a professional artist. She only knew that she had trouble sleeping, and that she slammed back and forth between states of depression and anxiety.

The unmanageable debt that she and Hawley had accrued over the last couple of years felt like a looming monster about to swallow them alive. Now they had both learned to recognize the Federal Reserve banking system as an even greater monster – a monster masquerading as their benefactor.

* * *

During her further Internet explorations, Brooke happened upon a message thread concerning John Hagli. It was located on a website called "squatloose", which purported to protect consumers against financial frauds and scams.

As she concentrated on this thread, Brooke began to realize that the 'regulars' at squatloose were totally convinced that John Hagli was a scam artist. Their posts were scathingly critical of both Hagli and the "debt elimination" process itself... especially its rationale.

They called people who believed in Hagli and his debt elimination process "moonbats", "fucktards", "deadbeats" and various synonyms for 'sucker'. They also challenged and insulted anyone who alluded to what they called "the vapor money theory".

Brooke also noticed a couple of adversaries arguing on Hagli's behalf... and a few detailed posts from Hagli himself. This was all very interesting reading.

She determined to examine both sides of this argument and make up her own mind. The best way to do that, she thought, would be to play 'Devil's Advocate'. So Brooke created a username for herself and began participating in the debt elimination debates on squatloose. For starters, she addressed the so-called "vapor money theory".

In her initial posts, Brooke presented herself as a desperate debtor who had come across information regarding debt elimination on the Internet. This was certainly true.

She questioned the squatloose group about the veracity of all the proposed debt elimination advice, as well as the information she'd learned concerning the Federal Reserve Banks -- especially their ability to create money out of thin air.

Initially, the squatloose group responded good-naturedly... presuming that Brooke was an easily-influenced victim of an attempted scam. But after she evinced too much knowledge concerning the subject of money creation, they became much less friendly.

During an exchange about the credit lending process, one of the squatloosers who called himself "Joey Blow", claimed that the banks actually lent out their depositors' funds: "...just like the Bailey Building and Loan in the movie *It's a Wonderful Life*", he wrote.

Brooke challenged this statement. She pointed out that one of the documents which used to be available on the Federal Reserve websites: *The Two Faces of Debt,* clearly described the Federal Reserve Banks' practice of creating "new money" whenever they lent "credit"... and she pointed out that this was a direct contradiction to Joey's assertion that the modern day banks lent out their depositors' pre-existing funds.

"If you had paid attention during "It's a Wonderful Life", Brooke wrote, "...you would have noticed that the Bailey Building and Loan was threatened because a healthy chunk of their depositors' actual savings had literally been removed from their savings accounts and physically lent out to other people in the community. This meant...", she continued, "...that in the event too many depositors sought to remove their funds, the bank would actually run out of funds on deposit before everyone could take out all of their money. This is what the word "bankrupt" really means -- the bank cannot return 100% of its deposits because a large percentage of these funds has actually been lent out."

"In George Bailey's final speech..." Brooke went on, "... he did his best to explain to all of his depositors that the survival of the Building and Loan, and the opportunity to earn interest on their deposited funds, depended upon a general willingness to leave most of their money in the bank together so that it could be lent out, and paid back over time, with interest. It took having faith in their own neighbors – the people who had borrowed the money."

"This is quite different from creating totally **new**, previously non-existent, 'vapor money' on behalf of a borrower... and then debiting **that** new account limit in order to pay for merchandise with nothing but an electronic credit to a merchant's bank account. It's all accomplished with a couple of bookkeeping entries."

Joey responded to this post by calling Brooke a "moron" and telling her that she needed to take a course in Economics 101.

Brooke pointed out that his insults were an indication that he knew nothing at all about economics himself... but could only resort to 'ad hominem' attacks because he was too short on facts -- a typical loser's debate tactic.

Then the other members of squatloose chimed in. They, too, insulted Brooke... questioned her intelligence... and generally attempted to convince her that she was too stupid to comprehend either the banking system or the Federal Reserve.

Shocked by the vehemence of this coordinated group attack Brooke decided that she needed to re-read Murray N. Rothbard's two books. She also decided to do some additional research before she responded to any further squatlooser posts.

Brooke had also noticed the name Dr. Edwin Vieira, Jr. mentioned by a couple of people who were taking her side during the debates... and the squatloosers attitude towards this man appeared equally scornful.... in spite of the fact that he held both a Juris Doctorate and a Phd. Now Brooke began to think that their attacks indicated desperation.

Brooke's research revealed that Dr. Edwin Vieira, Jr. had earned four degrees from Harvard: an A.B. (Harvard College); MA. and Ph.D. (Harvard Graduate School of Arts and Sciences), and J.D. (Harvard Law School).

On one website, Dr. Vieira's opinion was paraphrased thusly: "...that today's scheme of Federal-Reserve-System fiat currency and fractional-reserve banking is plainly un-constitutional, inherently fraudulent, economically unworkable in the long run, and subversive of America's political traditions of individual liberty and private property."

(http://www.citizensforaconstitutionalrepublic.com/Vieira _The_Federal_Reserve_System.html)

Everything Brooke discovered regarding Dr. Vieira's scholarly opinions, books, and speeches echoed and elucidated everything she had learned from reading the late Murray N. Rothbard. If anything, Dr. Vieira added a great deal of weight to the existing evidence.

It was sobering to contemplate that all these anonymous lawyers, judges, tax attorneys, and other supposed experts who populated the squatloose website could actually be deliberate apologists for a deceitful banking system... all the while posing as an anti-fraud squad trying to help the hapless consumer. Either that... or they, too, had been deluded by the obfuscations of a money-creation process which capitalized on the average citizens' ignorance.

About this time, the Plaintiff's surprisingly simple response to Brooke's Motion to Dismiss appeared in the mail:

RESPONSE TO DEFENDANT'S MOTION TO DISMISS

"COMES NOW the plaintiff, by and through undersigned counsel, and files this RESPONSE TO DEFENDANT'S MOTION TO DISMISS:

1. The key issues raised in the Motion to Dismiss are not grounds for dismissal as they involve alleged facts outside the four corners of the complaint.

2. The issues raised appear to be affirmative defenses."

That was it... *very* simple.

Now Brooke had a couple of new concepts to research: "affirmative defense", and "four corners of the Complaint".... and she had to do it quickly. There were only ten business days in which to file a new Reply in support of their Motion to Dismiss.

She was aware that she could extend this time by filing a NOTICE OF INTENT TO FILE A RESPONSE.

But that did not turn out to be necessary. Again, Brooke decided to turn to her paralegal friend Jeff for experienced help. She wisely realized that the two new concepts raised by the Plaintiff's attorney were still over her head.

He dutifully supplied her and Hawley with the following well-written response:

DEFENDANT'S SUPPORT FOR IT'S MOTION FOR DISMISSAL

COMES NOW the Defendant, Hawley Martin, to move this Honorable Court to dismiss the instant action for lack of jurisdiction pursuant to the terms of the agreement between the Plaintiff and the Defendant.

The Plaintiff has chosen to ignore the question as to the jurisdiction of this Honorable Court to hear this matter.

In <u>Schnurmacher Holding, Inc., v. Noriega</u>, 542 So. 2d 1327, (Fla 1989) the court stated:

As petitioner notes, the finality and enforceable nature of an arbitration award is a characteristic of arbitration that distinguishes it from other forms of alternative dispute resolution. To allow judicial review of the merits of an arbitration award for any reasons other than those stated in section 682.13(1) would undermine the purpose of settling disputes through arbitration. We find it incumbent to adhere to the long-standing principle of finality of arbitration awards in order to preserve the integrity of the arbitration process as a means of alternative dispute resolution.

CONCLUSION

Accordingly, the Plaintiff cites no authority for his proposition that a binding arbitration is merely an affirmative defense. The state of the law in Florida is such that the result of the arbitration is not subject to review by this Honorable Court, and, therefore, Plaintiff's abject failure to provide authority for jurisdiction in this Court.

This action should be dismissed for lack of jurisdiction.

About a week later, an envelope arrived from the Judge. To Brooke's great delight, it contained the following Order:

ORDER REQUIRING PLAINTIFF TO FILE MEMORANDUM OF LAW IN SUPPORT OF ITS RESPONSE TO DEFENDANT'S MOTION TO DISMISS

THIS CAUSE comes before the Court on Defendant's Motion to Dismiss and Memorandum of Law, filed with the Court on (date).

On (date) Plaintiff filed its Response to Motion to Dismiss. Thereafter on (date) Defendant filed Defendant's support for its Motion for Dismissal.

Defendant moves for dismissal for lack of jurisdiction pursuant to the terms of the arbitration agreement between the Plaintiff and Defendant.

Plaintiff asserts the Defendant's grounds for dismissal are improper and allege facts outside the four corners of the complaint. However, Plaintiff has failed to comply with this court's (date) Motion Practice Order.

> 2) Timely opposing memoranda. Each party opposing any written motion or other application shall file and serve, within ten (10) calendar days after being served with such motion or application, **a legal memorandum with citations to authority in opposition to the relief requested.** Failure to respond within the time allowed may be deemed sufficient cause for granting the motion by default.

Plaintiff's Response to Motion to Dismiss fails to include the appropriate memorandum of law in support of its motion. Therefore, after reviewing the file and the Motions, it is hereby:

ORDERED: Plaintiff upon receipt of this Order shall have ten (10) calendar days to file the appropriate Memorandum of Law in support of its Response to Motion to Dismiss.

Such an apparent act of fairness on the part of this Judge was encouraging. And it caused Brooke to pay **much** closer attention to the Judge's Motion Practice Order.

While she studied the concepts of "four corners of the complaint" and "affirmative defense", the Plaintiff apparently produced the required Memorandum of Law. Their amended response arrived:

PLAINTIFF'S MEMORANDUM OF LAW IN SUPPORT OF IT'S RESPONSE TO MOTION TO DISMISS

COMES NOW the Plaintiff, by and through undersigned counsel, and files this Memorandum of Law in Support of its Response to Defendant's Motion to Dismiss:

INTRODUCTION

Defendant has filed a motion to dismiss Plaintiff's complaint based on an allegation that he has already been awarded an arbitration award on the disputed amount. To support his motion, the Defendant has attached various exhibits. Plaintiff takes the position that the alleged arbitration award is not a proper basis for a motion to dismiss, and at best it is an affirmative defense.

ARGUMENT

In ruling on a motion to dismiss, the court can only look at the allegations within the four corners of the complaint (see McWhirter, Reeves et al v. Murray Weiss, attached). The court can only consider the exhibits attached to the complaint in ruling on a motion to dismiss (see City of Gainesville v. State of Florida, attached). In this case, it is clear that the defendant is introducing new arguments and exhibits that are not within the four corners of the complaint, or attached to it. As a matter of law, therefore, the court cannot consider the new arguments and exhibits while deciding the motion to dismiss.

While the Defendant may have an affirmative defense available to him, it cannot be used as the basis of a motion to dismiss (see Pizzi v. Central Bank and Trust, attached).

CONCLUSION

The court cannot consider the new issues and exhibits in deciding the Defendant's motion to dismiss. However, the Defendant will not be prejudiced by the denial of his motion, as he can raise the arbitration award as an affirmative defense.

———————————

Brooke found it extremely interesting to peruse the cited cases. She also noticed a URL at the bottom of each attached page:

http://www.versuslaw.com/research/resultDoc.aspx

When she attempted to surf to this URL, she was greeted with an invitation to subscribe to www.versuslaw.com. The monthly subscription was nominal – less than $20 per month – so she willingly signed up. Now she could conduct legal research from the comfort of her home office without having to drive downtown to the Court's Law Library and wade through physical books and indexes. This was exciting!

Even more exciting was the opportunity to find other applicable legal opinions within these same cases that the Plaintiff's attorney cited. For instance, in City of Gainesville v. State of Florida, she found the following opinion of the Florida Court of Appeal at paragraph [58]:

"Absent a written agreement, however, a vendor cannot sue the state for money damages on a contract theory."

She smiled to herself as she realized that the Plaintiff's attorney had neglected to provide a copy of any signed agreement between her and/or her husband and FunniBank in it's complaint. Did that mean that **all** written agreements were now "outside the four corners of the complaint"? Not **just** the arbitration agreement … but **any** alleged written agreement between the Hawley's and FunniBank? Perhaps this collections attorney had inadvertently provided Brooke with a proverbial "silver bullet".

But that particular bullet could be reserved for later. After enjoying her newly established monthly membership in an online legal research site, Brooke decided to continue pressing the issue of jurisdiction. She liked the feeling of storing up even better ammunition for later.

And there is nothing like exposing oneself to legalese from members of the BAR to hone one's own legal writing skills. Although she still relied upon her paralegal for the main body of the next Response, Brooke incorporated some of her own ideas on Hawley's behalf this time:

DEFENDANT'S RESPONSE TO PLAINTIFF"S MEMORANDUM

BACKGROUND

The Plaintiff and the Defendant had entered into a binding arbitration. The benefit of the arbitration was awarded to the Defendant herein. Part of the agreement upon entry into the arbitration was that it was binding upon both parties, and permitted no judicial review.

Plaintiff has filed a subsequent complaint omitting any mention of the prior arbitration award. Now plaintiff claims that the arbitration award is an "alleged fact outside the four corners of the complaint". By so doing, plaintiff attempts to disqualify any motion to dismiss which raises the issue of the pre- existing arbitration award. Thereby the very purpose of arbitration as an alternative dispute resolution could be sidestepped and undermined. Had plaintiff won said arbitration award, this complaint would never have been filed.

As stated previously, Defendant's motion to dismiss is brought for lack of jurisdiction. The plaintiff continues to ignore the question as to the jurisdiction of this honorable court to hear this matter.

DEFENDANT'S RESPONSE

The case of City Of Gainesville v. State, 778 So.2d 519, 778 So.2d 519 (Fla.App. 2001) is not supportive of counsels position, in that it involved the dual questions of sovereign immunity from taxation of the state by a city, but first whether it was in fact a tax being levied, or as applied, simply a use fee applicable to all properties for services rendered. Thus, in *Gainesville,* sovereign immunity must be viewed as an affirmative defense because it was not clearly dispositive of all jurisdictional issues. After all, the city of Gainesville *does* have a right to its use fees and to tax as its own sovereign. Therefore, the nature of the charge had to be determined prior to granting, or denying, the jurisdiction of the court.

In the case at bar, *Gainesville* is neither instructive nor controlling. The case at bar's jurisdictional denial stems from a **waiver** of judicial review upon completion of the arbitration process.

Similarly, Mcwhirter v. Murray ADD WEST CITE (2 DCA 1998) is off point, in that it is a case dealing with how a court must determine whether a motion to dismiss is valid in light of a claim of failure to state a cause of action. Not, as here, where the finality of an arbitration award acts as an estoppel to judicial review.

Plaintiff's reliance upon Pizzi v. Central Bank and Trust Company, 250 So. 2d 895 (Fla. 1971) is merely a regurgitation of the same irrelevant and immaterial argument. The Court has not been moved to dismiss the case at bar for failure to state a claim, but because the Plaintiff willingly entered into an agreement as a result of binding arbitration that is an estoppel to any further judicial review.

CONCLUSION

Plaintiff has attempted to sidestep the binding arbitration award by omitting to mention it within its complaint, and then seeking to confine Defendant's motion to the four corners of the complaint. Plaintiff has also attempted to focus the attention of the court upon whether not the existence of the arbitration award can also be raised as an affirmative defense. Plaintiff continues to ignore the proper question raised in Defendant's motion to dismiss as to the jurisdiction of this honorable court to hear a matter that has already been the subject of a binding arbitration award.

However, Defendant's motion to dismiss correctly relies upon authority upholding the finality and enforceable nature of an arbitration award as a means of alternative dispute resolution and estoppel to further judicial review.

WHEREFORE, this action should be dismissed for lack of jurisdiction.

Instead of feeling intimidated, Brooke felt empowered. She was learning to comprehend the legal rationale.

The next move in this game of strategy came from the Court -- another Order from the Judge:

ORDER TO SHOW CAUSE

THIS CAUSE comes before the court on Defendant's Motion to Dismiss and Memorandum of Law, filed with the Court on (date). On (date), Plaintiff filed its Response to Motion to Dismiss. Thereafter, on (date), Defendant filed Defendant's support for its Motion for Dismissal. On (date), the Court entered an Order requiring Plaintiff to file Memorandum of Law in support of its Response to Defendant's Motion to Dismiss. On (date), Plaintiff filed its Memorandum of Law in support of its Response to Motion to Dismiss. Subsequently, Defendant, on (date), filed its Response to Plaintiff's Memorandum of Law. Defendant moves for dismissal for lack of jurisdiction pursuant to the terms of the arbitration agreement between the Plaintiff and Defendant. After reviewing the file and the motions, it is hereby:

ORDERED: Plaintiff, upon receipt of this Order, shall have ten (10) calendar days to show cause as to why the Court should entertain jurisdiction in this matter, which has already been the subject of a binding arbitration award.

Forced to spend extra time on what he'd no doubt presumed would be another slam-dunk case against an easily intimidated and desperate debtor, the Plaintiff's attorney had to bring out his "big guns" now. His next response was thick, accusatory, and loaded with propaganda:

PLAINTIFF'S SHOWING OF GOOD CAUSE

COMES NOW the Plaintiff, by and through undersigned counsel, and files shows [sic] good cause as following [sic] as to why this case should not be dismissed for lack of jurisdiction:

1. Defendant filed a Motion to Dismiss the Complaint based on the allegation that he has already been awarded an arbitration award on the disputed account.

2. Defendant has not presented any grounds for the introduction of the alleged "arbitration award".

3. Arbitration is governed by contract and specific State Statutes.

4. Unless the Defendant produces an arbitration agreement which is a valid contract between the parties, and then shows that the procedures for arbitration contained in the agreement were followed, any "arbitration award" is void and meaningless.

5. Additionally, Plaintiff would allege the arbitration forum selected by Defendant is a sham organization, whose sole purpose is to award false and spurious "arbitration awards" to debtors.

6. Note that the outcome of the so called arbitration awarded the Defendant damages as the result and that neither party was present at the arbitration.

7. This Court has jurisdiction in this case to determine the validity of the arbitration award, and to hear the case if the arbitration award is invalid.

Attached were eight pages of single-spaced printouts obtained from various Internet sites dedicated to exposing and defending against several alleged "debt elimination scams"... including arguments against the "no money lent" argument, and descriptions of some supposedly "sham arbitration forums and awards".

Interestingly enough, it became apparent to Brooke that it was not the **existence** of the arbitration forums themselves that was supposedly bogus.

Anyone could legally become an "arbiter" if they were mutually acceptable to both parties in the proposed arbitration. Nowhere could Brooke find any established legal requirements for an "arbiter" or "arbitration forum".

There were procedural standards, and laws governing the length of time within which the arbitration must be completed, and for challenges to be filed, but no actual hard and fast **qualifications** had been established. Suggestions were offered as to professional backgrounds most suitable to the subject of the arbitration itself, but no actual certification or educational requirements seemed to exist.

The Credit Card companies had utilized arbitration forums of their own choice and preference against consumers for years... and some significant cases had already arisen from consumers' perception that these arbitration forums were dependant upon an enormous amount of business from the Credit Card companies for their very existence, and that **this** situation lent itself (pun intended) to a certain **bias** – a conflict of interest.

Any arbitration forums which issued awards in favor of consumers and against creditors were systematically attacked and sued by said creditors. This in and of itself created a conflict of interest so that the arbitration companies could no longer hear any arbitrations concerning those Plaintiff's which had filed suit against them.

They were put out of business by the all-powerful, deep-pocket banking and lending institutions whose persistent lawsuits bankrupted the small arbitration companies and prevented them from accepting any new assignments from any alleged customers of the accusing creditors.

Brooke began to see the overall situation as more of a guerilla war than a legitimate legal contest... especially after the way she had been treated on squatloose. This realization served only to make her more determined. Within a week's time, she composed and filed:

DEFENDANT'S REPLY TO PLAINTIFF"S SHOWING OF GOOD CAUSE AND MEMORANDUM OF LAW

COMES NOW the Defendant, Hawley Martin, in Reply to Plaintiff's Showing of Good Cause.

BACKGROUND

For valuable consideration which was accepted by Plaintiff on (date), 2004, Plaintiff and Defendant entered into an agreement to submit this matter to binding arbitration. Part of the agreement upon entry into the arbitration was that it was binding upon both parties, and permitted no judicial review.

Notice of Arbitration was delivered to Plaintiff on (date), 2004.

On (date), 2004, _____ Arbitrations Corporation mailed its Timeline Notice and Arbitration Committee Qualifications to the Plaintiff. A copy was sent to Defendant.

On (date), 2004, _____ Arbitrations Corporation mailed Plaintiff a follow up on its time line and notice to produce evidence. A copy was sent to Defendant.

Subsequently, an Arbitration Award was entered in favor of the Defendant herein on (date), 2004 and Plaintiff was notified thereof.

As of (date), 2004, the ninety (90) day period allowed by Florida Statute for either party to challenge the results of the Arbitration Award had elapsed.

Nevertheless, Plaintiff has filed a Complaint in this Honorable Court, which was served upon the Defendant on (date), 2004. This Complaint omitted any mention of the prior Arbitration Award. In fact, Plaintiff failed to allude to, allege, or even to mention the word "Jurisdiction" at any point within its Complaint.

Defendant filed its Motion to Dismiss for Lack of Jurisdiction on (date), 2004, citing the existence of the binding Arbitration Award.

Plaintiff then claimed that the binding Arbitration Award was an "alleged fact outside the four corners of the complaint", attempting to exclude any mention of it from this proceeding.

Defendant Replied that Jurisdiction had not been properly established, and that this tactic could sidestep and undermine the very purpose of binding arbitration as an alternative dispute resolution.

This Honorable Court issued its Order to Show Cause on (date), 2005, requiring Plaintiff to show cause as to why this Court should entertain Jurisdiction in this matter.

Now, having been forced to admit the existence of the binding Arbitration Award, and ordered to address the issue of Jurisdiction, Plaintiff has responded instead by attaching a slew of unsubstantiated allegations and hearsay concerning the Defendant, the arbitration forum, the arbiters, and the evidence allegedly submitted by Defendant to the arbitration committee, but nothing establishing the Jurisdiction of this Honorable Court.

Had Plaintiff wished to legitimately challenge the validity of the Arbitration Award, the arbitration forum, the arbitration process, the arbiters, or the evidence submitted by the Defendant, it had statutory opportunities to do so, which it has allowed to elapse and has therefore *waived.*

MEMORANDUM OF LAW

Plaintiff attaches two unmarked exhibits to its Showing of Good Cause. The first is dated (date), 2004, and the second is dated (date), 2004. Each exhibit details information known to the Plaintiff prior to the Notice of Arbitration delivered to Plaintiff on (date), 2004 and Defendant's Arbitration Award of (date), 2004. Plaintiff implies and alleges that such information might have applied to the arbitration agreement between the parties, and/or the arbitration forum chosen by the Defendant. These allegations are un-substantiated and groundless, and there are specified time periods during which either party may object to an agreement to arbitrate or to an arbitration, and raise any such questions about the authenticity thereof, see Florida Statutes 2004, Title XXXIX, Chapter 682:

682.03 Proceedings to compel and to stay arbitration:

(4) On application the court may stay an arbitration proceeding commenced or about to be commenced, if it shall find that no agreement or provision for

arbitration subject to this law exists between the party making the application and the party causing the arbitration to be had. The court shall summarily hear and determine the issue of the making of the agreement or provision and, according to its determination, shall grant or deny the application.

682.13 Vacating an award:

(2) An application under this section shall be made within 90 days after delivery of a copy of the award to the applicant, except that, if predicated upon corruption, fraud or other undue means, it shall be made within 90 days after such grounds are known or should have been known.

These 90 days elapsed as of (date), 2004.

Plaintiff also attempts to divert the Court's attention to various unsubstantiated allegations concerning the dispute(s) and/or argument(s) which it alleges that Defendant presented to the arbitration forum. Florida law has long upheld that findings of fact are left up to the arbitration committee, see: Florida Statutes 2004, Title XXXIX, Chapter 682:

682.03 Proceedings to compel and to stay arbitration:

(5) An order for arbitration shall not be refused on the ground that the claim in issue lacks merit or bona fides or because any fault or grounds for the claim sought to be arbitrated have not been shown.

The losing party in an Arbitration Award cannot object to the arbitrator(s) after suffering an adverse arbitration award, see: Dadeland Square, LTD. v. Gould, 763 So.2d 524, 763 So.2d 524 (Fla.App. 07/26/2000):

"...the trial court departed from the essential requirements of the law in granting Gould's motion to vacate the arbitration award because Gould waived the opportunity to question the arbitrator about his disclosed relationships and waived any

objection to the arbitrator until after Gould had suffered an adverse arbitration award."

"This Court has acknowledged and it is well-settled in federal courts that objections to the qualifications of arbitrators must be timely made and that the unsuccessful party in an arbitration proceeding cannot raise such an objection for the first time after the award is made. See Rios v. Tri-State Ins. Co., 714 So. 2d 547, 551 (Fla. 3d DCA 1998)."

Plaintiff cannot now claim to have had foreknowledge that an arbitration tribunal may be corrupt and then wait until it has suffered an adverse Arbitration Award to present such allegations, see: Technostroyexport v. International Dev. and Trade Serv., Inc., 139 F.3d 980 (2d Cir. 1998):

"...where party had knowledge of facts indicating that arbitration tribunal was corrupt prior to commencement of arbitration hearings but remained silent until adverse award was rendered, party waived its objection; Health Serv. Management Corp. v. Hughes, 975 F.2d 1253 (7th Cir. 1992)(objection of losing party in arbitration to award on basis of arbitrator's prior business relationships with prevailing party was waived as untimely); Swift Indep. Packing Co. v. District Union Local One, 575 F. Supp 912, 916 (N.D.N.Y. 1983)("In short, plaintiff made a calculated decision not to object to the alleged bias of Arbitrator Procopio and now seeks to avoid the consequences of what proves to have been a tactical error. Plaintiffs' 'belated cry of "bias" cannot now form a basis for setting aside the award; its silence constituted a waiver of this objection."

Also see: Ilios Shipping & Trading Corp., S.A. v. American Anthracite & Bituminous Coal Corp., 148 F. Supp 698, 700 (S.D.N.Y.), affirmed, 245 F.2d 873 (2d Cir. 1957):

"Where a party has knowledge of facts possibly indicating bias or partiality on the part of an arbitrator he cannot remain silent and later object to

the award of the arbitrators on that ground. His silence constitutes a waiver of the objection."

Finally, a Motion to Dismiss is an issue of law, not of fact. Plaintiff's attempt to introduce a slew of unsubstantiated allegations concerning Defendant's positions or the evidence Defendant may have presented to the arbitration forum are immaterial for purposes of ruling on the Jurisdiction of this Honorable Court. See: Expressway Companies, Inc. v. Precision Design, Inc., 882 So.2d 1016 (Fla.App. 07/14/2004):

"…a trial court "is not empowered to set aside arbitration awards for mere errors of judgment as to law or facts," even if Precision had filed a motion to modify the Award, the trial court could not have granted the motion. Dasso v. Fernandez, 831 So. 2d 714, 716 (Fla. 3d DCA 2002), review denied, 845 So. 2d 889 (Fla. 2003); see Verzura Constr., Inc. v. Surfside Ocean, Inc., 708 So. 2d 994, 996 (Fla. 3d DCA 1998) (holding that "awards made by arbitration panels cannot be set aside for mere errors of judgment either as to the law or as to the facts"); Goldberger v. Hofco, Inc., 422 So. 2d 898, 900 (Fla. 4th DCA 1982)

In Florida, arbitration is a favored means of dispute resolution and courts should indulge every reasonable presumption to uphold proceedings resulting in an award. See Roe v. Amica Mut. Ins. Co., 533 So. 2d 279, 281 (Fla. 1988). Review of arbitration decisions is extremely limited. See Boyhan v. Maguire, 693 So. 2d 659, 622 (Fla. 4th DCA 1997). A reviewing court may not comb the record of an arbitration hearing for errors of fact or law inherent in the decision-making process. See id. No provision in the Florida Arbitration Code authorizes trial judges to act as reviewing courts in the same way that a court of appeals reviews trial judges' legal decisions. See J.J.F. of Palm Beach, Inc. v. State Farm Fire & Casualty Co., 634 So. 2d 1089, 1090 (Fla. 4th DCA 1994). A high degree of conclusiveness attaches to an arbitration award because the parties themselves chose to go this route to avoid the expense and delay of litigation. See Applewhite v. Sheen Financial Resources, Inc., 608 So. 2d 80, 83 (Fla. 4th DCA 1992). The arbitrators are the sole and final judges of the evidence and the weight to be given it. See Verzura Constr., Inc. v. Surfside Ocean, Inc., 708 So. 2d 994 (Fla. 3d DCA 1998) (citing City of West Palm Beach v. Palm Beach County Police Benevolent Ass'n, 387 So. 2d 533, 534 (Fla. 4th DCA 1980)).

CONCLUSION

Plaintiff's Showing of Good Cause is a smokescreen of unsubstantiated allegations which should have been raised prior to the rendering of an Arbitration Award, and any legal action, motion or suit to review, modify or vacate the Arbitration Award should have been instigated within ninety (90) days thereafter.

Plaintiff fails to support its Showing of Good Cause with any Memorandum of Law, and it still fails to cite any authority whatsoever in support of the Jurisdiction of this Honorable Court to hear this matter.

Defendant correctly relies upon Florida Statutes specifying the parameters within which any questions concerning the arbitration agreement, arbitration forum and issues of fact should have been raised, and long-established authority upholding the finality and enforceable nature of a binding Arbitration Award as a means of alternative dispute resolution and estoppel to further judicial review.

WHEREFORE, this action should be dismissed for lack of jurisdiction.

The above response was filed by Brooke on the 9th of the month.

On the 22nd of the following month, a NOTICE OF PRODUCTION OF DOCUMENTS was filed by the Plaintiff, containing an attached copy of the alleged Cardholder Agreement, **unsigned by anyone**.

There was no attempt whatsoever to contradict any of the points asserted in Brooke's response. The alleged agreement included the usual Arbitration Clause insisting that any arbitration be conducted using one of the three arbitration forums chosen in advance by the Plaintiff.

On the 4th of the next month, the Judge ruled:

ORDER DENYING DEFENDANT'S MOTION TO DISMISS

THIS CAUSE comes before the Court on Defendant's Motion to Dismiss and Memorandum of Law, filed with the Court on (month) 24th, 2004. Defendant requests the Court to dismiss this action for lack of jurisdiction pursuant to agreement terms between the parties, specifically, Defendant's tender of final payment to Plaintiff, and an arbitration award.

The court, having reviewed the file and motion, notes that an arbitration award is an affirmative defense according to Florida rules of civil procedure 1.110(d). An affirmative defense may not be used as a basis for a motion to dismiss. Pizzi v. Central Park Trust, 250 So. 2d 895 (Fla 1971). Therefore, it is hereby

ORDERED: defendant's Motion to Dismiss is denied without prejudice.

After pondering this disappointing result for a bit, Brooke realized that she **should** have focused exclusively upon the **agreement** to arbitrate, which was **not** an "affirmative defense". She was learning… and the Judge's denial of her motion had been entered **without prejudice** – meaning that she could raise this issue again… and, hopefully, do it correctly.

But before trying that approach once more, Brooke thought she would surprise the Plaintiff by bringing up **other** valid matters which hadn't quite been cleared up:

The following were sent together by Certified Mail, on the 15th of the month:

DEFENDANT'S SECOND MOTION FOR MORE DEFINITE STATEMENT

DEFENDANT, Hawley Martin, moves this Honorable Court to enter an Order requiring Plaintiff to file a more definite statement of the complaint. In support of his motion, Defendant states as follows:

1. Plaintiff does not address or establish the jurisdiction of the Court in its complaint, as required by Rule 1.110 Florida Rules of Civil Procedure.

2. Account number XXXX XXXX XXXX XXXX would only have been opened following a credit card application and/or agreement signed by the applicant.

3. Any credit card application and/or agreement signed by the applicant would constitute a contract.

4. Plaintiff did not allege Breach of Contract in its Complaint.

5. Therefore, the complaint is ambiguous and it is not clear to the Defendant how to frame a responsive pleading.

6. The Plaintiff should be ordered, pursuant to Rule 1.140 Florida Rules of Civil Procedure, to state the complaint more definitely.

7. Or, in the alternative, the complaint should be dismissed in its entirety.

WHEREFORE the Defendant moves this Honorable Court to enter an Order requiring the Plaintiff to state the complaint more definitely, or, if Plaintiff fails or refuses to do so, dismissing the complaint with prejudice and granting such other and further relief as the Court may deem reasonable and just under the circumstances.

DEFENDANT'S FIRST REQUEST FOR ADMISSIONS

COMES NOW the Defendant, Hawley Martin, pursuant to Rule 1.370 Florida Rules of Civil Procedure, to request that Plaintiff, Funnibank (South Dakota), N.A. admit the truth of the following statements of fact:

1. Account number XXXX XXXX XXXX XXXX was opened following a credit card application and/or agreement signed by the applicant.

2. It is necessary for Defendant to have submitted a signed application and/or agreement before a credit card would have been issued by Plaintiff to Defendant.

3. Account number XXXX XXXX XXXX XXXX has been in existence for longer than one year.

4. Defendant has previously requested from Plaintiff, by mail, an authenticated copy of any credit card application and/or agreement signed by Defendant.

5. Plaintiff has thus far failed to provide Defendant with any copy whatsoever of any credit card application and/or agreement signed by Defendant.

6. Any credit card application and/or agreement signed by Defendant constitutes a contract.

7. Plaintiff did not allege Breach of Contract in its Complaint.

On the 22nd of the following month (over 37 days later) this Notice of Hearing arrived:

NOTICE OF HEARING

TO: HAWLEY MARTIN

YOU WILL PLEASE TAKE NOTICE that Defendant's 2nd Motion for More Definite Statement will be called up for Hearing at the MARION COUNTY COURTHOUSE AS FOLLOWS:

Judge: JOHN Q. JUSTICE

Date: *(over 90 days **later** than this Notice!)*

Time: 10:00 am* (or as soon thereafter as counsel may be heard)

*COUNSEL FOR PLAINTIFF WILL APPEAR TELEPHONICALLY .

15 minutes have been reserved for this hearing.

PLEASE GOVERN YOURSELF ACCORDINGLY.

But as of 19 days after this Notice of Hearing arrived, the following Order to Show Cause was received – much to Brooke and Hawley's surprise and delight:

ORDER TO SHOW CAUSE

THIS CAUSE comes before the Court on Defendant's Second Motion for More Definite Statement, filed with the Court (date). After reviewing the Motion and the file, it is hereby

ORDERED: Plaintiff, upon receipt of this Order, shall have ten (10) calendar days to show cause as to why the Court should not grant Defendant's Second Motion for More Definite Statement.

DONE AND ORDERED in chambers in XXXXX, Florida, this XXst day of XXXXX, 200X.

Encouraged by the Judge's apparent willingness to make the Plaintiff's attorney 'tow the line', Brooke decided to pursue Discovery. She had studied discovery tactics from Jurisdictionary and was eager to put them into practice.

She filed the following Discovery Request seven days after they received their copy of the Judge's Order to Show Cause (over two months prior to the supposedly scheduled Hearing):

DEFENDANT'S SECOND REQUESTS FOR ADMISSION

COMES NOW the Defendant, Hawley Martin, to request that Plaintiff, FunniBank (South Dakota), N.A. admit the truth of the following statements of fact pursuant to Rule 1.370 Florida Rules of Civil Procedure: "Without leave of Court the request may be served upon the Plaintiff after commencement of the action", and Rule 1.050: "Every action of a civil nature shall be deemed commenced when the complaint or petition is filed".

To: FunniBank (South Dakota) N.A. (please note: where discovery requests are directed to a corporation, counsel for the corporation is required to nominate officers of the corporation to answer).

Definitions

a. "You" and "your" include FunniBank (South Dakota) N.A. and any and all persons acting for or in concert with FunniBank (South Dakota) N.A.

b. "Document" includes every piece of paper held in your possession or generated by you.

Instructions

1. These requests for admissions are directed toward all information known or available to FunniBank (South Dakota) N.A. including information contained in the records and documents in FunniBank (South Dakota) N.A.'s custody or control or available to FunniBank (South Dakota) N.A. upon reasonable inquiry. Where requests for admission cannot be answered in full, they shall be answered as completely as possible and incomplete answers shall be accompanied by specific reasons for the incompleteness of the answer, including specification of whatever actual knowledge **is** possessed with respect to each unanswered or incompletely answered request for admission.

2. Each request for admission is to be deemed a continuing one. If, after serving an answer to any request for an admission, you obtain or become aware of any further information pertaining to that request for admission, you are requested to serve a supplemental answer setting forth such information.

3. As to every request for an admission which you fail to answer in whole or in part, the subject matter of that admission will be deemed confessed, admitted and stipulated as fact to the Court.

Defendant, Hawley Martin, submits the following requests for admission to Plaintiff FunniBank (South Dakota) N.A. You are required to answer each request for admission separately and fully, in writing, under oath, and to serve a copy of the responses upon Hawley Martin within thirty (30) days after service of these requests for admissions, or they shall be deemed admitted.

1) Admit that FunniBank (South Dakota) N.A. is not licensed to do business in Florida by virtue of being registered with the Secretary of State and nominating an agent for service of process.

Response:

2) Admit that FunniBank (South Dakota) N.A. has no regular, systematic way of doing business in Florida, (also known as "minimum contacts") as would be evidenced by such things as yellow pages listings for FunniBank (South Dakota) N.A and logos appearing at retail outlets clearly signing "FunniBank (South Dakota) N.A."

Response:

3) Admit that Pat Answers, PA has purchased evidence of debt from the named Plaintiff: FunniBank (South Dakota), N.A, and is proceeding with collection activity in the name of the original owner of the account: FunniBank (South Dakota), N.A.

Response:

4) Admit that FunniBank (South Dakota) N.A. is not the present holder of a contract with Hawley Martin.

Response:

5) Admit that FunniBank (South Dakota) N.A. possesses no account and general ledger statement verifying that Hawley Martin presently owes FunniBank (South Dakota) N.A. any money.

Response:

6). Admit that notice of dispute of Defendant's account number XXXX XXXX XXXX XXXX was served by the Defendant on/or about (month) of 2004.

Response:

7) Admit that Defendant's check in the amount of $20.00 was enclosed with Defendant's first letter of dispute mailed to Plaintiff on (month) 25th, 2004.

Response:

8) Admit that Defendant's check in the amount of $20.00 was specifically identified within said letter of dispute and marked as final payment on account number: XXXX XXXX XXXX XXXX.

Response:

9) Admit that the above mentioned letter of dispute, mailed to Plaintiff on (month) 25th, 2004, also specifically identified the above-mentioned $20.00 check as consideration for the Plaintiff's agreement to arbitrate.

Response:

10) Admit that Defendant's dispute letter mailed to Plaintiff on (month) 25th, 2004 included the following written statement: "Your acceptance of my final payment and agreement to binding arbitration waives your right to maintain any lawsuit against us in any Court".

Response:

11) Admit that Plaintiff raised no objection to the proposed arbitration.

Response:

12) Admit that Defendant's $20.00 check which was enclosed with Defendant's letter of dispute, notice of final payment and agreement to arbitrate was cashed by Plaintiff on (month) 29th, 2004.

Response:

13) Admit that Defendant's "Notice of Arbitration: XXXX XXXX XXXX XXXX" was received by Plaintiff on (next month) 15th, 2004 in Sioux Falls, SD 57117.

Response:

14) Admit that Plaintiff made no objection to the arbitration agreement between Plaintiff and Defendant, the

arbitration forum, or the arbiters after receiving Notice of Arbitration.

Response:

15) Admit that Plaintiff chose not to participate in the arbitration, even though it was noticed at all times of all proceedings.

Response:

16) Admit that an Arbitration Award regarding the disputed account # XXXX XXXX XXXX XXXX was rendered in favor of the Defendant and against the Plaintiff by Champlain Valley Arbitrations Corporation on (next month) 20th, 2004.

Response:

17) Admit that Plaintiff made no objection to the arbitration agreement between Plaintiff and Defendant, the arbitration forum, or the arbiters prior to the entry of the Arbitration Award.

Response:

18) Admit that Plaintiff made no objection to the Arbitration Award within 90 days following rendering and notice of the Arbitration award.

Response:

19) Admit that Florida case law holds that one who chooses not to participate in binding arbitration, and does not raise timely objection, is bound by the arbitration award.

Response:

20) Admit that a binding arbitration award is not reviewable by any Court.

Response:

END OF DEFENDANT'S SECOND REQUESTS FOR ADMISSION

_____

Also filed on the same date as above:

_____

DEFENDANT'S FIRST REQUEST FOR PRODUCTION OF DOCUMENTS

COMES NOW, the Defendant, Hawley Martin, pursuant to the Florida Rules of Civil Procedure, Rule 1.280: "(1) In General. Parties may obtain discovery regarding any matter, not privileged, that is relevant to the subject matter of the pending action, whether it relates to the claim or defense of the party seeking discovery or the claim or defense of any other party, including the existence, description, nature, custody, condition, and location of any books, documents, or other tangible things and the identity and location of persons having knowledge of any discoverable matter. It is not ground for objection that the information sought will be inadmissible at the trial if the information sought appears reasonably calculated to lead to the discovery of admissible evidence", and Rule 1.350: "(b) Procedure. Without leave of Court the request may be served on the Plaintiff after commencement of the action", and Rule 1.050: "Every action of a civil nature shall be deemed commenced when the complaint or petition is filed.

All documents requested herein are directly and specifically relevant to the subject matter of the pending cause of action, and are or should be kept in the normal course of Plaintiff's business activities. Plaintiff is requested to disclose and produce all documents requested, and send verified, authenticated photocopies of all discovery to Defendant. Plaintiff is required to furnish such information as is available to Plaintiff, Plaintiff's agents, or officers possessing first-hand knowledge of the events or documents in question.

If Plaintiff cannot respond in full to any request for production of documents after making reasonable efforts to secure the required information, respond to the extent possible and set forth the efforts Plaintiff has made to secure the required information.

Plaintiff shall produce all of the requested documents on or before thirty (30) days from the receipt of this request.

DEFINITIONS

a. "You" and "your" include FunniBank (South Dakota) N.A. and any and all persons acting for or in concert with FunniBank (South Dakota) N.A.

b. "Document" includes every piece of paper held in your possession or generated by you.

c. General Ledger is defined as: "The ledger that contains all of the financial accounts of a business; contains offsetting debit and credit accounts (including control accounts) - American Heritage Dictionary of the English Language, Fourth Edition, published by Houghton Mifflin Company.

To: FunniBank (South Dakota) N.A.

Defendant, Hawley Martin, submits the following request for production of documents to Plaintiff FunniBank (South Dakota) N.A. If the document does not exist, you are required to state that it does not exist.

Failure to comply fully or partially with this request within thirty days of receipt of service shall be deemed a confession that the document does not exist and/or that FunniBank (South Dakota) N.A. is committing fraud by concealment.

INSTRUCTIONS

1. These requests for production of documents are directed toward all information known or available to FunniBank (South Dakota) N.A. including information contained in the records and documents in FunniBank (South Dakota) N.A.'s custody or control or available to FunniBank (South Dakota) N.A. upon reasonable inquiry. (Please note: where discovery requests are directed to a corporation, counsel for the corporation is required to nominate officers of the corporation to answer).

2. Each request for production of documents is to be deemed a continuing one. If, after serving an answer to any request for an admission, you obtain or become aware of any further information pertaining to that requested production of documents, you are requested to serve a supplemental answer setting forth such information.

REQUESTS FOR PRODUCTION
OF DOCUMENTS

1. All pages, front and back, of the FunniBank (South Dakota) N.A. corporate charter.

2. A certified copy of the original certificate of authority that allows the named Plaintiff, FunniBank (South Dakota) N.A. to do business in the state of Florida.

3. The account and general ledger pertaining to each and every contract that FunniBank (South Dakota) N.A. alleges that Hawley Martin has established with FunniBank (South Dakota) N.A.; showing all receipts and disbursements; verified under penalty of perjury by an employee of FunniBank (South Dakota) N.A.

4. An authenticated copy, front and back, verified under penalty of perjury by an employee of FunniBank (South Dakota) N.A., of any contract and/or agreement signed by Defendant, Hawley Martin, which Plaintiff FunniBank (South Dakota) N.A. alleges that Defendant established with Plaintiff.

5. An authenticated copy, front and back, verified under penalty of perjury by an employee of FunniBank (South Dakota) N.A., of any and all assignments or allonges of any existing contract or agreement with Plaintiff that was signed by Defendant, Hawley Martin.

6. An authenticated copy, front and back, verified under penalty of perjury by an employee of FunniBank (South Dakota) N.A, of the contract for services which FunniBank (South Dakota) N.A has established with Patrick A. Carey, P.A.

7. An authenticated copy, front and back, verified under penalty of perjury by an employee of FunniBank (South Dakota) N.A, of any agreement authorizing Pat Answers, P.A. to act in the capacity of Plaintiff's attorney representing FunniBank (South Dakota) N.A. in the above-captioned action.

Two days later, Plaintiff's Reply to Request for Admissions came in the mail – it had been filed the day after Brooke's two Discovery Requests had been mailed to the Court. They had probably crossed in the mail:

REPLY TO REQUEST FOR ADMISSIONS

COMES NOW THE PLAINTIFF, by and through undersigned counsel, and files this reply to Defendant's request for admissions:

1. Unknown at this time, therefore, denied.

2. Denied

3. Admitted

4. Admitted

5. Admitted

6. Admitted

7. Admitted.

And there were more items in this large envelope. There was also a personal letter from a different Collections Attorney:

"Dear Counselor:

Attached Please find an amended complaint that I have filed in this case. I believe it addresses the issues raised in your Second Motion for More Definite Statement, and therefore I believe it would be appropriate for you to file an answer to it, pursuant to Rule 1.190(a).

Should you have any questions, do not hesitate to contact me.

Ms Muffett (a different Atty)

This is a communication from a debt collector."

Next came the Plaintiff's:

SHOWING OF GOOD CAUSE

COMES NOW the Plaintiff, by and through undersigned counsel, and shows good cause as to why Defendants Second Motion for More Definite Statement should not be granted, and in support thereof states that Plaintiff has filed an Amended Complaint addressing the issues raised in Defendant's Motion.

Plaintiff therefore moves this Court for an Order denying Defendant's Motion for More Definite Statement.

And finally, the Amended Complaint:

AMENDED COMPLAINT

Plaintiff sues Defendant(s) and alleges:

    1. This is an action for damages in the amount of $_____

    2. The Court has jurisdiction over the subject matter, which is a suit for money damages only and the parties, due to the fact the Plaintiff is a national bank who transacts business in said county, and the Defendant(s) entered into the agreement between the parties, which is the subject matter of this lawsuit, in said county and/or is a resident of said county.

    3. Venue is proper in the above stated county as the Defendant(s) entered into the agreement between the parties, which is the subject matter of this lawsuit, in said county and/or is a resident of said county.

    4. Plaintiff is a national bank, governed by the national bank act, and as such is exempt from filing a non-resident cost bond, and is also authorized by Florida law to file and maintain this lawsuit.

    5. Plaintiff is a national bank, governed by the National Bank Act, and as such is exempt from Florida's usury statutes. *(NOTE: isn't it convenient that our helpful representatives in Congress enacted national legislation to sidestep the State's usury statutes?!)*

    6. All conditions precedent to filing this lawsuit have been met.

Count I

    7. Plaintiff realleges and reincorporates into this count all preceding paragraphs.

    8. Plaintiff established a credit card account for the Defendants at Defendant's request.

    9. Plaintiff issued one or more credit cards to the Defendants.

10. Defendants made or authorized certain purchases using the credit cards; said purchases were charged to credit account established by Plaintiff.

11. Defendants have not paid the balance due on the credit card account.

12. Defendants owe Plaintiff $_____, which is due with interest as the balance due on the account, as reflected on the account statements attached as Composite Exhibit "A".

13. A copy of the credit agreement, Which includes a provision for an attorney fee, in the event of collection litigation, and is attached as exhibit "B".

14. By the Defendant's acceptance and use of the credit card issued by Plaintiff, there was an acceptance of the terms of the credit agreement referenced above.

WHEREFORE, Plaintiff demands judgment against the Defendants in the sum of $_____ together with costs, interest, and such other relief as the Court may deem just and proper.

Count II

15. Plaintiff realleges and reincorporates into this count paragraphs one through six, above.

16. Defendant owes Plaintiff $_____ which is due with interest as the balance due on an Open Account, as reflected on the documentation attached as Plaintiffs composite exhibit "A".

WHEREFORE, Plaintiff demands $_____ together with costs, interest, and such other relief as the Court may deem just and proper.

Count III

17. Plaintiff realleges and reincorporates into this count paragraphs one through six, above.

18. Before the institution of this action Plaintiff and Defendant had business transactions between them and they agreed to the resulting balance.

19. Plaintiff rendered a statement of it to Defendant, a copy being attached as exhibit "C", and Defendant did not object to the statement.

20. Defendant owes Plaintiff $_____, which is due with interest, on the account.

WHEREFORE, Plaintiff demands judgment against the Defendant in the sum of $_____, together with costs, interest, and such other relief as the Court may deem just and proper.

The above Amended Complaint included all the attachments described within.

Meanwhile, Brooke noticed that her **First** Requests for Admission had not been answered by the Plaintiff within the legally specified time period... and according to statute they could now be "deemed admitted" by default. But she had to **move** the Court to do so. Jurisdictionary had informed her that the Court will do **nothing** that it is not moved to do by one or the other parties to the action:.

MOTION TO HAVE DEFENDANT'S FIRST REQUESTS FOR ADMISSION DEEMED ADMITTED

Comes now, the Defendant, Hawley Martin, to move this Honorable Court to deem Defendant's First Requests for Admission admitted by Plaintiff.

1) Defendant propounded its First Requests for Admission to Plaintiff on **(month) 15th, 2005.**

2) Plaintiff failed to respond to Defendant's First Requests for Admission until **(two months later) 8th, 2005.**

3) Florida Rules of Civil Procedure, Rule 1.370, requires the responding party to file its Response **within thirty (30) days** or the Requests for Admission may be deemed admitted.

WHEREFORE, Plaintiff did not file its Response to Defendant's First Requests for Admission for **over fifty-three (53) days**, Defendant's First Requests for Admissions should be deemed admitted.

And on that same day, Brooke also mailed her:

DEFENDANT'S REPLY TO PLAINTIFF'S SHOWING OF GOOD CAUSE

AND

MOTION TO DISMISS THIS ACTION

OR RENDER JUDGMENT BY DEFAULT

AGAINST THE PLAINTIFF

(DISOBEDIENT PARTY)

Comes now, Defendant, Hawley Martin, in Reply to Plaintiff's Showing of Good Cause to state his reasons why Plaintiff should still be required to amend its Complaint according to the reasons enumerated in Defendant's Motion for More Definite Statement. Additionally, because of Plaintiff's repeated failure to obey this Court's Order(s) and the Florida Rules of Civil Procedure, Defendant now moves this Honorable Court to dismiss this case in its entirety, **or** to render judgment by default against the Plaintiff (disobedient party), according to the provisions of this Honorable Court's Order to Respond and Motion Practice Order.

ARGUMENT

1) Defendant filed its Motion for More Definite Statement on **(month) 15th, 2005**. Plaintiff failed to respond to this Motion within the parameters set forth by this Honorable Court's Order to Respond and Motion Practice Order issued in November of 2004; to wit:

> **"2)** *Timely opposing memoranda.* **Each party opposing any written motion or other application shall file and serve, <u>within ten (10) calendar days</u> after being served with such motion or application, a legal memorandum with citations to authority in opposition to the relief requested. <u>Failure to respond within the time allowed may be deemed sufficient cause for granting the motion by default</u>.** *If a party has no objection to a motion and does not intend to file a responsive memorandum, counsel shall file a written notice with the clerk of the Court so indicating."*

a) Plaintiff failed to file **any** Response within the required ten (10) calendar days. In fact, Plaintiff allowed this time period to elapse by **over thirty (30) days**, and then set the matter for hearing without first consulting with the Defendant. Please see exhibit "AA" (Notice of Hearing – date of service highlighted in yellow). Plaintiff's action disregarded this Court's Order to Respond and Motion Practice Order as follows:

> **"6)** *Oral argument.* **Motions and other applications will ordinarily be determined by the Court on the basis of motion papers and legal memoranda <u>unless a hearing is required by rule or law</u>. (For example, under the rules, summary judgment motions should be set for hearing. This would not, however, extinguish the requirement that the motion be accompanied by and responded to with memoranda.)**

"When a request for hearing is granted, counsel for the requesting party will be asked to coordinate the calendars of the Court and counsel."

b) On **May 20th, 2005**, Defendant was served a NOTICE OF HEARING by council for the Plaintiff, without coordinating the calendars of the Court and counsel, and accompanied by no legal memoranda. Counsel for the Plaintiff apparently hoped that this Court would allow him to ignore its orders, set a hearing over twenty days after his time to respond had elapsed, and then sit back in his office chair to argue the motion telephonically for 15 minutes without preparing any legal memoranda whatsoever. Meanwhile he expected the Defendant to miss work, jeopardize his employment, and attempt to defend his Motion orally within a mere fifteen (15) minute time period. This would have seriously compromised the Defendant's ability to adequately reply on his own behalf. As a Pro Se litigant the Defendant needs time to consider the Plaintiff's arguments and to perform legal research before replying with the required legal memoranda.

Defendant was preparing a Motion to Cancel this Hearing based upon the parameters of this Court's Order to Respond and Motion Practice Order, when Defendant received his copy of this Court's Order (to the Plaintiff) to Show Cause why this Court should not grant Defendant's Motion for More Definite Statement.

2) Defendant also served his First Requests for Admission on the Plaintiff (month) 15th, 2005. Plaintiff failed to respond within the thirty (30) day period prescribed by Florida Rules of Civil Procedure, Rule 1.370:

"The matter is admitted unless the party to whom the request is directed serves upon the party requesting the admission a written answer or objection addressed to the matter within 30 days

after service of the request or such shorter or longer time as the Court may allow..."

a) In fact the Plaintiff served its belated reply to Defendant's Requests for Admission on (month) 8, 2005 – twenty-three (23) days **after** the thirty (30) day period had elapsed. This Court has not indicated any intention to allow a longer period of time before the fact.

3) Plaintiff has also filed two false and misleading Certificates of Service with its Amended Complaint and its belated Reply to Request for Admissions. They each read:

"CERTIFICATE OF SERVICE

I HEREBY CERTIFY that a true and correct copies [sic] of the foregoing **and Plaintiff's affidavit in support of its Motion for Summary Judgment** was furnished to:

Hawley Brooke

P.O. BOX XXX

XXXXX, FL

by U.S. Mail Delivery on X/8/05. This is a communication from a debt collector.

Ms Muffett, P.A."

a) NO such affidavit in support of any Motion for Summary Judgment was **ever** furnished to the Defendant. The above quoted Certificates of Service are false. Please see Exhibits "BB" and "CC". If this Honorable Court has received any such Motion for Summary Judgment from the Plaintiff, and/or any such affidavit in support of such a Motion for Summary Judgment from the Plaintiff, the Defendant has never received **either** such document and is completely unaware of the filing of either such document.

4) Plaintiff continues to disrespect this Honorable Court and the Defendant by ignoring this Court's Order to Respond and

Motion Practice Order. Said Order of this Court includes the following admonition:

"FAILURE OF EITHER PARTY TO COMPLY WITH THE TERMS OF THIS ORDER MAY RESULT IN THE STRIKING OF PLEADINGS OR PARTS OF THEM OR STAYING FURTHER PROCEEDINGS UNTIL THIS ORDER IS OBEYED OR DISMISSING THE ACTION OR RENDERING JUDGMENT BY DEFAULT AGAINST THE DISOBEDIENT PARTY."

WHEREFORE Plaintiff has habitually failed to act within the requirements of this Court's Order to Respond and Motion Practice Order, and the Florida Rules of Civil Procedure, and such actions are considered reason for the granting of the opposing party's Motion, or dismissal of the offending party's case, or rendering judgment by default against the disobedient party, Defendant so moves this Honorable Court to dismiss this case with prejudice or to render judgment by default against the disobedient party and in favor of the Defendant.

1VERIFICATION

Defendant certifies that he has read this Reply and Motion(s) set forth herein, and that to the best of his knowledge, information and belief, formed after reasonable inquiry, believes that they are well-grounded in fact and warranted by existing law, and that they are not imposed for any improper purpose such as unnecessary delay, or to harass, or to needlessly increase the cost of litigation.

DATED this _____ day of _____ 2005

_____

The **next** day an envelope arrived containing a Judge's order denying our Second Motion for More Definite Statement... no doubt because the Plaintiff had filed its Amended Complaint:

ORDER DENYING DEFENDANT'S SECOND MOTION FOR MORE DEFINITE STATEMENT

THIS CAUSE came before me upon Defendants Second Motion for More Definite Statement, and good cause being shown as to why the Motion should be denied, and the Court being fully advised in the premises, it is therefore ORDERED AND ADJUDGED that Defendant's Motion is denied.

On the same day that this Judge's order was entered, Brooke had also mailed her two Motions. No doubt they had crossed in the mail.

She also noticed an interesting detail about the envelope that contained this Order. It was not the same kind of official envelope with the Judge's full name and return address embossed in the upper left-hand corner... it was an ordinary blank envelope, with a sloppily applied, pre-printed address label stuck in the center bearing Hawley's name and PO Box address. Each of the previous Judge's Orders had arrived in an official Court envelope and had been neatly addressed to Hawley in longhand.

Brooke concluded that *this* Order and pre-addressed envelope had been pre-prepared and enclosed with the Amended Complaint by the Plaintiff's attorney, so that the Judge could sign it immediately. This is a tactic recommended by Jurisdictionary, and Brooke could easily see why. It spared the Judge from preparing it him/herself... and convenience counts.

The Judge had apparently signed this Order before receiving Brooke's two Motions, which had both been filed within the time limit allotted by law for a Reply.

Brooke did not intend to take this lying down. Her next pleading was even more unfriendly... and it was in the mail only four days later...

CHAPTER SEVEN

Open Waters

With this next set of pleadings, Brooke and Hawley finally wriggled free of the Plaintiff's 'hook':

DEFENDANT'S MOTION TO RESCIND THIS COURT'S ORDER DENYING DEFENDANT'S SECOND MOTION FOR MORE DEFINITE STATEMENT,

AND TO CONSIDER DEFENDANT'S TIMELY REPLY TO PLAINTIFF'S SHOWING OF GOOD CAUSE

Comes now, Defendant, Hawley Martin, to submit his Motion to Rescind this Court's Order Denying Defendant's Second Motion for More Definite Statement and to consider Defendant's Timely Reply to Plaintiff's Showing of Good Cause due to the premature issuance of the above referenced Order by this Honorable Court.

BACKGROUND

Defendant's Reply was mailed to this Court on (month) 14th, 2005 and apparently crossed in the mail with this Court's Order Denying Defendant's Second Motion for More Definite Statement, which was also mailed on (month) 14th, 2005. That Order of this Court was issued and mailed only four (4) official days after the Plaintiff finally served its Showing of Good Cause in response to this Court's Order to Show Cause.

This Court's earlier Order to Respond and Motion Practice Order of (month) 2004 prescribes five (5) additional days to be allowed for a moving party's final Reply to the opposing party's Response before the Court's ruling on a Motion, provided that written notice of intent to Reply is received by the Court. But rather than submit any written notice of intent to Reply, Defendant actually served his Reply within the five (5) days extra time to be allowed for mailing, as per Florida Rules of Civil Procedure Rule 1.090:

> (a) Computation. In computing any period of time prescribed or allowed by these rules, by order of Court, or by any applicable statute, **the day of the act, event, or default from which the designated period of time begins to run shall not be included**. The last day of the period so computed shall be included unless it is a Saturday, Sunday, or legal holiday, in which event the period shall run until the end of the next day which is neither a Saturday, Sunday, or legal holiday. **When the period of time prescribed or allowed is less than 7 days, intermediate Saturdays, Sundays, and legal holidays shall be excluded in the computation**.

> (e) **Additional Time After Service by Mail**. When a party has the right or is required to do some act or take some proceeding within a prescribed period after the service of a notice or other paper upon that party and the notice or paper is served upon that party by mail, **5 days shall be added to the prescribed period**.

Plaintiff's Showing of Good Cause was mailed on (month) 8th, 2005, which was a Wednesday. As provided by Rule 1.090, that day is to be excluded from the computation of time. Two days, Thursday and Friday, then elapsed; followed by Saturday and Sunday, which are also to be excluded from calculation. The Court's Order Denying Defendant's Second Motion for More Definite Statement was mailed on Tuesday, (month) 14th. That Tuesday and the Monday preceding it make two additional days, for a total of only four (4) days to be lawfully included in the computation of time. By mailing his Reply to Plaintiff's Showing of Good Cause, etc. on Tuesday, (month) 14th, 2005, this Defendant served his actual Reply on this Honorable Court within the extra five (5) days which are to be allowed for mailing.

Defendant prays that this Honorable Court has no intention of holding the Defendant to a standard of conformity to its rules and orders that is different from that which is expected of the Plaintiff in this case.   Therefore, Defendant now moves this Court to rescind its premature Order Denying Defendant's Second Motion for More Definite Statement and to consider Defendant's Reply to Plaintiff's Showing of Good Cause.

Due to the fact that this Court issued its Order Denying Defendant's Second Motion for More Definite Statement prematurely, Defendant was not allowed sufficient time to serve his Reply prior to this Court's ruling on his Motion for More Definite Statement.

Plaintiff should still be required to amend its Complaint according to each of the reasons enumerated in Defendant's Motion for More Definite Statement, because, although the Plaintiff did amend its Complaint as to the requirement of the Florida Rules of Civil Procedure requiring the Plaintiff to allege the Jurisdiction of this Court, the Plaintiff's Amended Complaint **still** fails to allege the existence of any signed agreement or contract between the Plaintiff and the Defendant, and fails to attach any copy of such contract or agreement to its Complaint.

By virtue of its failure to object to or deny Defendant's First Requests for Admission within thirty (30) days, the following Requests for Admission pertaining to the necessity of such a contract (served on Plaintiff {month} 15th, 2005) should now be deemed admitted:

1) Account number XXXX XXXX XXXX XXXX   was opened following a credit card application and/or agreement signed by the applicant.

2) It is necessary for Defendant to have submitted a signed application and/or agreement before a credit card would have been issued by Plaintiff to Defendant.

3) Account number XXXX XXXX XXXX XXXX has been in existence for longer than one year.

4) Defendant has previously requested from Plaintiff, by mail, an authenticated copy of any credit card application and/or agreement signed by Defendant.

5) Plaintiff has thus far failed to provide Defendant with any copy whatsoever of any credit card application and/or agreement signed by Defendant.

6) Any credit card application and/or agreement signed by Defendant constitutes a contract.

7) Plaintiff did not allege Breach of Contract in its Complaint.

Defendant served his First Requests for Admission on the Plaintiff (month) 15th, 2005. Plaintiff failed to respond within the thirty (30) day period prescribed by Florida Rules of Civil Procedure, Rule 1.370:

> **"The matter is admitted unless the party to whom the request is directed serves upon the party requesting the admission a written answer or objection addressed to the matter within 30 days after service of the request or such shorter or longer time as the Court may allow..."**

In fact the Plaintiff served its belated reply to Defendant's Requests for Admission on (month) 8th, 2005 – twenty-three (23) days after the thirty (30) day period had elapsed. This Court has not indicated any intention to allow a longer period of time before the fact. Therefore, the above Requests for Admissions being deemed admitted, Plaintiff should be required to allege the existence of a contract in its Complaint.

ARGUMENT

1) Defendant filed its Motion for More Definite Statement on **(month) 15th, 2005**. Plaintiff failed to respond to this Motion within the parameters set forth by this Honorable Court's Order to Respond and Motion Practice Order issued in November of 2004; to wit:

> **"2) *Timely opposing memoranda.* Each party opposing any written motion or other application shall file and serve, <u>within ten (10) calendar days</u> after being served with such motion or application, a legal memorandum with citations to authority in opposition to the relief requested. <u>Failure to respond within the time allowed may be deemed</u>**

sufficient cause for granting the motion by default. *If a party has no objection to a motion and does not intend to file a responsive memorandum, counsel shall file a written notice with the clerk of the Court so indicating."*

a) Plaintiff failed to file **any** Response within the required ten (10) calendar days. In fact, Plaintiff allowed this time period to elapse by **over thirty (30) days**, and then set the matter for hearing without first consulting with the Defendant. Please see exhibit "AA" (Notice of Hearing – date of service highlighted in yellow). Plaintiff's action disregarded this Court's Order to Respond and Motion Practice Order as follows:

"6) O*ral argument.* Motions and other applications will ordinarily be determined by the Court on the basis of motion papers and legal memoranda <u>unless a hearing is required by rule or law</u>. (For example, under the rules, summary judgment motions should be set for hearing. This would not, however, extinguish the requirement that the motion be accompanied by and responded to with memoranda.)

"When a request for hearing is granted, counsel for the requesting party will be asked to coordinate the calendars of the Court and counsel."

b) On **(month) 20th, 2005**, Defendant was served a NOTICE OF HEARING by council for the Plaintiff, without coordinating the calendars of the Court and counsel, and accompanied by no legal memoranda. Counsel for the Plaintiff apparently hoped that this Court would allow him to ignore its orders, set a hearing over twenty days after his time to respond had elapsed, and then sit back in his office chair to argue the motion telephonically for 15 minutes without preparing any legal memoranda whatsoever. Meanwhile he expected the Defendant to miss work, jeopardize his employment, and attempt to defend his Motion orally within a mere fifteen (15) minute time period. This would have seriously compromised the Defendant's ability to adequately reply on his own behalf. As a

Pro Se litigant the Defendant needs time to consider the Plaintiff's arguments and to perform legal research before replying with the required legal memoranda.

2) Plaintiff continues to disrespect this Honorable Court and the Defendant by ignoring this Court's Order to Respond and Motion Practice Order. Said Order of this Court includes the following admonition:

> "FAILURE OF EITHER PARTY TO COMPLY WITH THE TERMS OF THIS ORDER MAY RESULT IN THE STRIKING OF PLEADINGS OR PARTS OF THEM OR STAYING FURTHER PROCEEDINGS UNTIL THIS ORDER IS OBEYED OR DISMISSING THE ACTION OR RENDERING JUDGMENT BY DEFAULT AGAINST THE DISOBEDIENT PARTY."

WHEREFORE Plaintiff has habitually failed to act within the requirements of this Court's Order to Respond and Motion Practice Order, and the Florida Rules of Civil Procedure Rule 1.090 regarding TIME, and such actions are considered reason for the granting of the opposing party's Motion, or dismissal of the offending party's case, or rendering judgment by default against the disobedient party, Defendant so moves this Honorable Court to either grant Defendant's Second Motion for More Definite Statement or to dismiss this case or to render judgment by default against the disobedient party and in favor of the Defendant. 2

VERIFICATION: Defendant certifies that he has read this Reply and Motion(s) set forth herein, and that to the best of his knowledge, information and belief, formed after reasonable inquiry, believes that they are well-grounded in fact and warranted by existing law, and that they are not imposed for any improper purpose such as unnecessary delay, or to harass, or to needlessly increase the cost of litigation.

DATED this _____ day of _____ 2005. Respectfully submitted, Hawley Martin

_____

Three days later, Brooke also filed the following:

DEFENDANT'S AMENDED
REPLY TO PLAINTIFF'S SHOWING OF GOOD CAUSE

Comes now, Defendant, Hawley Martin, to Amend and clarify his Reply to Plaintiff's Showing of Good Cause and to state his reasons why Plaintiff should still be required to amend its Complaint according to EACH and EVERY reason enumerated in Defendant's Motion for More Definite Statement.

BACKGROUND

1)   Defendant filed its Motion for More Definite Statement on **(date) 15th, 2005**. Plaintiff failed to respond to this Motion within the parameters set forth by this Honorable Court's Order to Respond and Motion Practice Order issued in November of 2004; to wit:

"2)   *Timely opposing memoranda.* Each party opposing any written motion or other application shall file and serve, <u>within ten (10) calendar days</u> after being served with such motion or application, a legal memorandum with citations to authority in opposition to the relief requested. <u>Failure to respond within the time allowed may be deemed sufficient cause for granting the motion by default.</u> *If a party has no objection to a motion and does not intend to file a responsive memorandum, counsel shall file a written notice with the clerk of the Court so indicating.*"

a)   Plaintiff failed to file **any** Response within the required ten (10) calendar days. In fact, Plaintiff allowed this time period to elapse by **over thirty (30) days**, and then set the matter for hearing without first consulting with the Defendant. Please see exhibit "AA" (Notice of Hearing – date of service highlighted in yellow). Plaintiff's action disregarded this Court's Order to Respond and Motion Practice Order as follows:

> **"6) *Oral argument.* Motions and other applications will ordinarily be determined by the Court on the basis of motion papers and legal memoranda <u>unless a hearing is required by rule or law</u>. (For example, under the rules, summary judgment motions should be set for hearing. This would not, however, extinguish the requirement that the motion be accompanied by and responded to with memoranda.)**

> **"When a request for hearing is granted, counsel for the requesting party will be asked to coordinate the calendars of the Court and counsel."**

b) On **May 20th, 2005**, Defendant was served a NOTICE OF HEARING by council for the Plaintiff, without coordinating the calendars of the Court and counsel, and accompanied by no legal memoranda. Counsel for the Plaintiff apparently hoped that this Court would allow him to ignore its orders, set a hearing over twenty days after his time to respond had elapsed, and then sit back in his office chair to argue the motion telephonically for 15 minutes without preparing any legal memoranda whatsoever. Meanwhile he expected the Defendant to miss work, jeopardize his employment, and attempt to defend his Motion orally within a mere fifteen (15) minute time period. This would have seriously compromised the Defendant's ability to adequately reply on his own behalf. As a Pro Se litigant the Defendant needs time to consider the Plaintiff's arguments and to perform legal research before replying with the required legal memoranda.

c) Defendant was preparing a Motion to Cancel this Hearing based upon the parameters of this Court's Order to Respond and Motion Practice Order, when Defendant received his copy of this Court's <u>Order</u> (to the Plaintiff) <u>to Show Cause</u> why this Court should not grant Defendant's Motion for More Definite Statement.

2) In response to this Court's Order to Show Cause the Plaintiff filed its Showing of Good Cause along with an Amended Complaint on **June 8th, 2005**. In its Showing of Good Cause, Plaintiff claims to have addressed "...the issues raised in Defendant's Motion" by filing its Amended Complaint. But Defendant asserts that Plaintiff did **not** address **all** of the issues raised in Defendant's Motion for More Definite Statement. **In fact, Plaintiff's Amended Complaint continues to dodge the issue of the signed application and agreement (contract) which would have been necessary for Plaintiff to issue a credit card to the Defendant.** The fact that such a signed application and agreement would have been required should be deemed admitted because Defendant's First Requests for Admission were not objected to or denied within the thirty (30) days specified by Florida Rules of Civil Procedure, Rule 1.370.

3) Defendant served his First Requests for Admission on the Plaintiff April 15th, 2005. Plaintiff failed to respond within the thirty (30) day period prescribed by Florida Rules of Civil Procedure, Rule 1.370:

> **"The matter is admitted unless the party to whom the request is directed serves upon the party requesting the admission a written answer or objection addressed to the matter within 30 days after service of the request or such shorter or longer time as the Court may allow..."**

a) In fact the Plaintiff served its belated reply to Defendant's Requests for Admission on (date) 8, 2005 along with its Amended Complaint – twenty-three (23) days after the thirty (30) day period allowed to respond to the Requests for Admission had elapsed. This Court has not indicated any intention to allow any such longer period of time before this fact.

4) Therefore, by virtue of its failure to object to or deny Defendant's First Requests for Admission within thirty (30) days, the following seven (7) Requests for Admission (served on Plaintiff {date} 15th, 2005) pertaining to the necessity of such a signed application, agreement and contract should now be deemed admitted:

1) Account number XXXX XXXX XXXX XXXX was opened following a credit card application and/or agreement signed by the applicant.

2) It is necessary for Defendant to have submitted a signed application and/or agreement before a credit card would have been issued by Plaintiff to Defendant.

3) Account number XXXX XXXX XXXX XXXX has been in existence for longer than one year.

4) Defendant has previously requested from Plaintiff, by mail, an authenticated copy of any credit card application and/or agreement signed by Defendant.

5) Plaintiff has thus far failed to provide Defendant with any copy whatsoever of any credit card application and/or agreement signed by Defendant.

6) Any credit card application and/or agreement signed by Defendant constitutes a contract.

7) Plaintiff did not allege Breach of Contract in its Complaint.

5) The above seven (7) Requests for Admission having been deemed admitted, the **Plaintiff should have to amend its Complaint to make a more definite statement alleging the existence of such a contract, and attach a verified copy thereof to its Complaint**.

6) Plaintiff has also filed two false and misleading Certificates of Service with its Amended Complaint and its belated Reply to Request for Admissions. They each read:

"CERTIFICATE OF SERVICE

I HEREBY CERTIFY that a true and correct copies [sic] of the foregoing **and Plaintiff's affidavit in support of its Motion for Summary Judgment** was furnished to

HAWLEY MARTIN

P.O. BOX XXX, (town) FL XXXXX-XXXX

by U.S. Mail Delivery on X/8/05.

This is a communication from a debt collector.

PAT ANSWERS, P.A."

a) Defendant states under oath that NO such affidavit in support of any Motion for Summary Judgment was **ever** furnished to the Defendant. The above quoted Certificates of Service are **false**. Please see Exhibits "BB" and "CC". If this Honorable Court has received any such Motion for Summary Judgment from the Plaintiff, and/or any such affidavit in support of such a Motion for Summary Judgment from the Plaintiff, the **Defendant has never received either such document and is completely unaware of the filing of either such document**. Defendant does not know whether or not these two (2) false Certificates of Service were accidental or deliberate.

7) Plaintiff continues to disrespect this Honorable Court and the Defendant by ignoring this Court's Order to Respond and Motion Practice Order. Said Order of this Court includes the following admonition:

> **"FAILURE OF EITHER PARTY TO COMPLY WITH THE TERMS OF THIS ORDER MAY RESULT IN THE STRIKING OF PLEADINGS OR PARTS OF THEM OR STAYING FURTHER PROCEEDINGS UNTIL THIS ORDER IS OBEYED OR DISMISSING THE ACTION OR RENDERING JUDGMENT BY DEFAULT AGAINST THE DISOBEDIENT PARTY."**

WHEREFORE Plaintiff has habitually failed to act within the requirements of this Court's Order to Respond and Motion Practice Order, and the Florida Rules of Civil Procedure, and such actions are considered reason for the granting of the opposing party's Motion, or dismissal of the offending party's case, or rendering judgment by default against the disobedient party, Defendant so moves this Honorable Court to dismiss Plaintiff's case, or render judgment by default against the Plaintiff (disobedient party) or admit into the record and consider this Amended Reply to Plaintiff's Showing of Good Cause before ruling on Defendant's Second Motion for More Definite Statement.

VERIFICATION

Defendant certifies that he has read this Reply and Motion(s) set forth herein, and that to the best of his knowledge, information and belief, formed after reasonable inquiry, believes that they are well-grounded in fact and warranted by existing law, and that they are not imposed for any improper purpose such as unnecessary delay, or to harass, or to needlessly increase the cost of litigation.

DATED this _____ day of _____ 2005

Respectfully submitted, Hawley Martin

_____

As repetitive and tedious as this whole process obviously was, it was absolutely necessary in order to prevail in the end.

Six days later, the Martins received their copy of the Plaintiff's latest responses.

First:

REPLY TO DEFENDANT'S REQUEST FOR PRODUCTION

COMES NOW THE PLAINTIFF, by and through undersigned counsel, and files this reply to Defendant's Request for Production:

1. Objection, burdensome, improper, relevance, not reasonably calculated to lead to admissible evidence.

2. Objection, improper, burdensome, relevance and not reasonably calculated to lead to admissible evidence.

3. objection, improper, burdensome, relevance and not a reasonably calculated to lead to admissible evidence.

4. objection as to authenticated, verified copies as improper, burdensome, relevance and not reasonably calculated to lead to admissible evidence. Plaintiff has already provided a copy of the cardholder agreement, *see complaint*. Application not available at this time.

5. objection as to authenticated, Verified copies as improper, burdensome, relevance and not reasonably calculated to lead to admissible evidence. Objection as to relevance and question is vague and confusing.

6. objection improper, burdensome, relevance and not reasonably calculated to lead to admissible evidence, attorney-client privilege, and work product.

7. objection, improper, relevance and not reasonably calculated to lead to admissible evidence.

Next:

REPLY TO DEFENDANT'S SECOND REQUEST FOR ADMISSION

COMES NOW THE PLAINTIFF, by and through undersigned counsel, and files this reply to Defendants second request for admission:

1. Objection improper and relevance.

2. Objection improper and relevance.

3. Deny that Plaintiff's attorney purchased evidence of debt. Plaintiff's attorney is representing Plaintiffs in this proceeding. Deny remainder.

4. Deny.

5. Objection improper, relevance and form of question.

6. Objection. Vague and unknown as to which document Defendant refers. Defendant failed to attach the documentation to the request pursuant to Florida rules of civil procedure 1.370.

7. Admit that Defendants sent a payment in the amount of $20.00 To Plaintiff, which was received on or about (date). *See statements filed with the Court.* Denied as to remainder as information is unknown at this time.

8. Objection. Defendant failed to attach the documentation to the request pursuant to Florida roles of civil procedure 1.370.

9. Unknown at this time, therefore denied.

10. Pursuant to the letter dated (date), which is attached to Defendant's motion to dismiss, Plaintiff admits that said letter contains that sentence. Deny as to remainder.

11. Deny. *See cardholder agreement.*

12. Objection. Defendant failed to attach the doc-umentation to the request pursuant to Florida rules of civil procedure 1.370.

13. Objection. Defendant failed to attach the doc-umentation to the request pursuant to Florida rules of civil procedure 1.370.

14. Deny. *See cardholder agreement.*

15. Admit as to participation. Deny as to remainder.

16. Admit.

17. Deny. *See cardholder agreement.*

18. Deny. *See cardholder agreement.*

19. Objection to form of question, vague and relevance.

20. Deny.

Yet **another** photocopy of the alleged Cardholder Agreement was attached.

Two weeks later, the Judge issued one more Order which apparently placed too great a burden of proof on the opposition:

ORDER TO RESPOND

THIS CAUSE comes before the Court on Defendants amended reply to Plaintiffs showing of good cause, filed with the Court on (date). Defendant raises several issues regarding motion practice order violations and untimely discovery responses. After reviewing the file it is hereby

ORDERED: Plaintiff, within fifteen calendar days of the date of service of this order, shall respond to the issues raised in Defendants amended reply to Plaintiffs showing of good cause.

DONE AND ORDERED in Chambers in XXXX, XXXXX County, Florida this XXth day of (month), 200X.

(signature)

JOHN Q. JUSTICE

Circuit Court Judge

That did it.

One month and a day later this case was officially **closed.**

Plaintiff's counsel filed a **Notice of Voluntary Dismissal** rather than respond to the Defendant's latest Motions.

No final notice of dismissal was ever mailed to the Martins. They only learned that the case had been dismissed by checking their local Clerk of the Court website.

Apparently this Collections Attorney chose not to announce his retreat.

<><<<>>><>

EPILOGUE

As of now, April of 2009, it has been almost five years since the Defendants enjoyed this satisfying little victory.

The **Statute of Limitations** has run out on all four banks' right to file a lawsuit for collection of unsecured debt here in Florida.   This is because there has been **NO activity whatsoever on any of the Defendants' alleged credit cards or alleged debt accounts since March of 2004.**

Any dunning letters and annoying phone calls are merely efforts to fish for any alleged debtors who are unaware of the Statute of Limitations. These letters and phone calls are literally made by computers, which print out the letters and/or dial the telephone numbers. **Only** after someone responds – either by sending a letter back, or by picking up the phone and saying "Hello" – will an actual, flesh and blood human being ever become involved.

It is extremely important to realize that **making any signed agreements whatsoever with any alleged former lender or collector after the SOL has run out will cause the SOL to reset again from the very beginning!!!**

THIS salient fact explains why collectors continue to harass supposed debtors for years after the SOL has already run out on these supposed debts. They HOPE to fish out those potential defendants who are ignorant of the law.

It takes only ONE charge on the credit card, or ONE check written in payment of a past alleged debt, or ONE signature on ONE proposed settlement offer to reset the SOL and afford the collectors several more years (the SOL period varies from State-to-State) in which to serve you with a lawsuit.

Even though their statutory time period for filing a case has elapsed, they will often persist in both harassments and enticements designed to fool you into **somehow,** accidentally resetting the SOL.

The enticements are particularly devious. They may offer dramatic reductions in the amount of the original alleged debt, and point out that the unpaid debt has damaged your credit rating, hoping you will assume that your credit rating will be improved after accepting an agreement to settle. **NOT SO!!!**

On the contrary... the presence of any record of settlement constitutes admission of responsibility for the debt, will continue to impact your FICA score, and the dollar difference between the original amount and the amount settled for will ALSO be **reported as income to you on a 1099 MISC** for the tax year in which the settlement was made.

ALL SORTS of arguments and persuasions might be presented to you in an effort to get you to use that credit card, and/or wring some amount of payment out of you, and get that SOL started all over again.

Another little-known fact is that telephone debt collectors are constrained by strict regulations against revealing any embarrassing financial information about any alleged debtors to any third party (Fair Debt Collection Practices Act). Therefore, should any stranger call you and ask for you by name, **do not** reveal it. Instead, ask the caller who **they** are. If it **is** a debt collector, they will usually repeat the full name of the person whom they are trying to contact, and will ask you again if you are that person.

Never reveal your identity to any strange callers. Instead, ask them for **their** name again and inquire as to the nature of their business. They will often become uncomfortable and act impatient and impolite... and will avoid revealing the reason for their call; insisting upon speaking to the person they requested. If pressed further about who they are and what company they represent, they might reveal that it is a personal business matter between themselves and the person they are trying to contact. If that happens, you can be quite sure that you are speaking to a debt collector.

I occasionally receive one of those annoying calls... and they always begin with: "Heidi?" or: "Are you Heidi Guedel?" (they usually mispronounce my last name).

My reply is ALWAYS: "Who's THIS?" and the rest of the conversation goes something like:

Them: "We are trying to reach Heidi Guedel. Are you Heidi Guedel?

Me: "Who are *YOU?*"

Them: "I am Steve from (collection firm)."

Me: "Why did you call this number?"

Them: "I have an important business call for Heidi Guedel. Are you Heidi? Do you know Heidi?"

Me: "I'm sorry, but I never reveal personal information to strangers. I need to know your exact name, the company you work for, and the precise nature of your business."

Them: "We can only discuss this matter with Heidi. This is a confidential business matter. *Are you Heidi?*"

Me: "You seem to be avoiding my question. Who are you and what is your business? You called this number... so you tell me the nature of your business."

Them: (usually becoming irritated and impatient) "I've already told you, I can only discuss this matter with Heidi Guedel. **Are YOU HEIDI???"**

Me: "What if I said I *WAS* Heidi.... how would you know I was telling you the *truth?*"

Them: "I would ask you to verify certain personal information, such as your social security number; your mother's maiden name, and your date of birth... and only after you've answered everything correctly would I discuss this important matter with you."

Me: "Oh ... I *see*.... well... how do I know you're not just some phone scammer on some fishing expedition to find out enough data to commit identity theft???"

Them: (exasperated) "This conversation is over." (sometimes they just hang up at this point).

That's the basic technique.... have fun with it. Always refuse to reveal your identity until they have revealed theirs, and have also revealed the exact nature of their business.

They can't. 8-)

Be well, be wise, and be careful.

Printed in the United States
218751BV00006B/49/P

9 780557 066209